Edgar Fawcett

A Romance of Old New York

Edgar Fawcett

A Romance of Old New York

ISBN/EAN: 9783744666022

Printed in Europe, USA, Canada, Australia, Japan

Cover: Foto ©Thomas Meinert / pixelio.de

More available books at **www.hansebooks.com**

A ROMANCE OF OLD NEW YORK

A ROMANCE OF OLD NEW YORK

BY

EDGAR FAWCETT

PHILADELPHIA & LONDON
J. B. LIPPINCOTT COMPANY
1897

A ROMANCE OF OLD NEW YORK.

I.

THE two young men had just turned a corner of State Street, and had come full into view of the Battery, green and breezy, with its flashes from the broad bay beyond, glimpsed between foliage of maple and elm.

"Good-morning, Mr. Burr."

"Good-morning, sir; good-morning."

Mark Frankland raised his hat, and the short, slender gentleman with the clear-cut face and large, dark-blue, sparkling eyes saluted him in like way, though somewhat more ceremoniously.

Mark's friend gave a little annoyed shrug. "How can you treat that man with such respect?" he said, a note of scorn in his voice.

Mark made no reply till they had both seated themselves on a bench in the great verdurous common. Over them leaned a tree whose boughs turned the vivid May sunshine into twinkling arabesques of gold.

"I was somehow brought up," said Mark Frankland, stretching his shapely limbs, which were tired after hours spent in his merchant father's office near by on South Street,—"I was somehow brought up, Gerald, to treat Aaron Burr like a gentleman."

"Humbug!" scoffed Gerald Suydam. "He isn't a gentleman. He's a horrible scoundrel, and you know it! That Blennerhassett business dyes him black as one, and then his duel with Hamilton——"

"Oh, I know just what you're going to say," broke in Mark, dashing his cambric kerchief over a dust-spot on the sleeve of his cinnamon-colored coat. "Dad has his ideas about all the outrageous buncombe printed and talked on the subject of Hamilton, and so have I. The truth is, Gerald, that Alexander Hamilton, with all his talents and virtues, was very far from being a saint."

"And thousands of people are willing to swear that Aaron Burr is very near to being a devil."

"The masses are nearly always wrong," said Mark, staring down at one of the burnished buttons on his low-cut "Washingtonian" waistcoat. "As you know, Colonel Burr is a welcome guest at my father's house, and often drops in there to supper of an evening."

"Oh, I know," nodded Gerald Suydam, with a smile of polite disapprobation. "The countenance of your family, Mark, has been a decided feather in his cap. When Burr returned from his four years' absence abroad, in 1812, it was for some time an actual disgrace to be seen in his company. Now, eight years later, in 1820, his position would not be much better but for the civility shown him by certain of our leading townsfolk."

With furtive amusement Mark scanned his companion's face.

"Mr. Varick Verplanck happens to be among these, Gerald."

"Oh, yes; I grant it."

Mark laid a hand on Gerald's

shoulder. His voice, usually careless, deepened; an unwonted gravity
sobered his brightness.

"I know, Gerald, how your people
hold him in abhorrence. But dad
and Mr. Verplanck are right. Burr,
for a man of his splendid intellect,
has done madly foolish things."

"Foolish, eh?"

"Oh, come, now. If his Blennerhassett scheme had succeeded, if he
had made himself Aaron I., Emperor
of Mexico, and his young grand-
child, Aaron Burr Alston, heir pre-
sumptive to the throne, with his
daughter, Theodosia, an imperial
princess, with General Wilkinson
commander-in-chief of the army,
and with Blennerhassett minister to
England,—if he had accomplished,
I say, this melodramatic, filibuster-
ing purpose, we would to-day be
praising his brilliant capacities, and

forget the fact of his having shot in a duel the man who for years abused and assailed him both with tongue and pen. After all, we must remember, even our great Washington was a rebel——"

"But not a traitor," sharply struck in Gerald.

"He'd have been hanged as one if the British had caught him—hanged with hardly more ceremony than they showed our poor Nathan Hale when they strung him up on that apple-tree in old Rutgers Orchard, now the junction of Market Street and East Broadway. All rebels, my dear Gerald, are looked upon as traitors —till they succeed."

"I hate, Mark, to hear you compare Burr with Washington. It positively sickens me!" And Gerald Suydam folded his arms with a look of defiance on his dark, virile face.

"Nonsense!" admonished Mark, lifting a forefinger. "Nobody reveres and honors Washington's memory more than do I. He was a man infinitely above Burr in *morale*, I admit, though I doubt if in real mental power he equalled him."

"Idiocy—rank idiocy!" breathed Gerald.

"Thanks, old fellow. I don't mind having an intimate friend tell me, now and then, that I'm a fool. It rather wakes me up to a healthful sense of my own deficiencies."

"Now, Mark, you know very well that I didn't mean——"

"Oh, of course you didn't. There —shake hands. You've never met Burr; you've never been under the marvellous spell of his magnetic personality. I have, Gerald. I've heard him tell of those four years he spent abroad—from 1808 till 1812 —as an exile and a wanderer. The tears have flooded my eyes while I listened. Though received with delighted graciousness by the most distinguished citizens of London, Edinburgh, Stockholm, Hamburg, Gotha, Weimar, and finally Paris, his sufferings in those foreign lands were terrible past belief. Almost everywhere he was an object of governmental suspicion and distrust——"

"Naturally."

"Well, yes, naturally, I concede. But his torments of poverty would have wrung the stoniest heart. Think of it! A man who had been, but a few years before, Vice-President of the United States, and had come within an ace of being our President, subsisted for weeks at a time, in Paris, on a few francs a day! And not only had he to fight this form of hardship. The government of Napoleon kept him under incessant surveillance, and his efforts to quit the shores of France were for months agonizingly delayed. At last he did escape, after thwartings and rebuffs that might have driven to madness a spirit less resolute and cheerful. He landed here in New York secretly and by night. The same torments of poverty still dogged him, and to these the odium was added of nearly every one who recognized him as Aaron Burr. But with indomitable pluck and nerve he resumed the practice of law—a profession, you will grant, in which, during former years, he had shone superb and almost unique. And then, scarcely a year later, came the crushing blow of his adored daughter's death. And such a death! The Charleston steamer which bore Theodosia Alston to the father whose worship she had always so devotedly returned never reached this port. You recall the harrowing stories, Gerald, of its having been boarded by pirates, and of Theodosia's unknown yet possibly terrific fate."

"Oh, yes. I remember. Who does not?"

"Burr bore this ghastly affliction with mighty stoicism. A great light went out of his life, but he permitted no one to see the awful darkness which followed there. Since then he has striven to rise above the crushing effects of his bereavement, and such effort does him honor, in its dignity, calmness, and reserve. He may not always have been a good man, but he surely knows how to suffer like a true one!"

"Oh," laughed Gerald, though not quite amiably, "here's enthusiasm run riot! I see that Burr has mesmerized you; they say he can do it with both men and women, though especially the latter."

"You end your sentence with a sneer," said Mark Frankland. "But let me tell you that nearly all Burr's reported gallantries are the coinage of his relentless enemies."

"Do you mean to say——?" began Gerald, rather hotly.

"I mean to say that he has always had a native and peculiar power of charming women. He is now in his sixty-fourth year, and yet scarcely less vigorous and healthful than if he were five-and-thirty. His manner, to every woman he meets, young or old, comely or plain, is the essence of courtesy, jollity, admiration, and delicate tact. Hence all sorts of bugaboo tales are circulated concerning his sorry licentiousness."

"Would you care to have him pay his courtly compliments to your sister," asked Gerald, with smouldering obstinacy, "provided you had a sister?"

Mark rose, stretching his legs and arms, and giving his smart attire a few dainty touches.

"Lord 'a mercy, man," he said, "I've seen him hold a silk skein for my sweetheart by the half-hour at a time, and deliberately get it all of a tangle, and whisper pretty things to her with a roguish look at myself, and set her laughing like an April brook and blushing like a June rose, and I've never any more dreamed of feeling jealous of him than if he'd been my great-grandfather."

"By your sweetheart," said Gerald, rising also and following his friend, "you of course mean Charlotte Verplanck."

"Whom else *could* I mean?" replied Mark, with a slight inflection of haughty surprise. "Surely you know that we've been engaged for more than a fortnight."

"Oh, yes, I know. You . . told me, you remember. Besides, I had drawn my inferences."

Gerald murmured these words in an abstracted way. His eyes were lowered upon the path beneath him, and he stroked his chin with nervous fingers.

Mark made no answer. He looked very happy and genial, there in the vernal light, under the variant shadows of waving trees.

"Perhaps you've noticed," Gerald went on, slow-voiced and with an accent of melancholy, "that I never go up yonder any more."

Mark started. He understood at once that "up yonder" meant the big brick mansion of Mr. Varick Verplanck, on Broadway, only a block or two beyond the grassy circle of Bowling Green.

"Yes," he said, a little awkwardly, "I *have* noticed that you've given up visiting Pamela."

Gerald lifted his head, now, with an exasperated sigh. "Look here, Mark. I wanted to tell you something when we began our little walk. But your enthusiastic eulogy of Colonel Burr kept it back. I don't suppose you will like to hear it, but I can't help that."

"Not like to hear it? Why, is it anything so very disagreeable?"

"Yes; it has relation to Pamela's

illness. They say she has become a very sick girl."

"She isn't at all well, certainly. Charlotte is anxious about her sister, and so is Mr. Verplanck."

"They say, Mark, that the girl is rapidly going into a decline."

"I trust it's nothing so bad as that, Gerald. Though Charlotte and her father are both worried, still, only yesterday, Dr. Wainwright told him that he thought it a trouble of the nerves, and that it might not prove at all serious. They're going to take her off into the country soon —to their place at Throgg's Neck, you know. You and I have spent some pleasant hours there, in recent summers, have we not?"

"Yes, Mark, when I believed Pamela Verplanck cared for me. But now it's clear to my mind that she has never cared."

"And I suppose you still want her to care?" said Mark, slowly.

"Want her to care! Good God, man, why don't you ask me if I want her to be dying of love for *you?*"

Mark turned like a flash, and the two faced one another.

"Who's been telling you, Gerald, such rubbish as this?"

"Never mind. It has come from a credible source."

"From the gabbling tongues of gossips." Mark's blue eyes were ablaze, and his lips had curled in a sneer.

Gerald looked sorrowful but firm. "I believe it is true," he said. Then a stormy grief stamped every feature, and his voice became vibrant with tremors that he plainly sought to hide. "Past observations confirm it now. Certain of her acts and words recur to me . . . Oh, Mark,"—he broke off, with a great burst of vehemence,—" if this were true of any other living man but yourself I should hate him—I should feel like killing him! But we've been friends from boyhood —we were college classmates—we shared each other's likings and sports and scrapes and troubles; we're distant kinsmen by blood, but brothers in affection, sympathy. I can't hate you—no, I can't!"

Mark saw the tears glitter in his friend's big, dusky eyes. Gerald flung himself on a bench near by, and sat there, his lithe young body swerved sideways, biting his lips and clenching both hands.

Mark walked on, pausing at the water's edge. He felt horribly shocked at Gerald's late words. A vision of Charlotte Verplanck, the girl he loved and meant to marry, rose before him, with her plump yet lissome shape, her damask cheeks, her ropes of crinkled blue-black hair. Then came a vision of her sister, Pamela, once the rosiest and winsomest of blondes, now sallow and languid, with half her beauty gone and the pallor as of mortal sickness replacing it.

A shiver passed through Mark; a sense of gruesome omen darkened the luminous May air. Yet his look was stubborn, rebellious, incredulous, as he murmured, half aloud,—

"It isn't true—it can't be true. Pamela dying of love for me! Old women's tea-table tattle! And Gerald has listened to it! Well, all the bigger fool he. There always *was* a babyish, hysterical streak in Gerald, despite his many manly and honest traits!"

II.

MARK stood for some time on the very verge of the Battery, either watching or seeming to watch the hazy blue of the Staten Island hills and the sparkle of the Narrows and the glimmering curve of the Jersey coast. These looked then, no doubt (seventy-five years ago), much the same as they have often looked on pleasant afternoons of our own later springtides. But the bay was far less full of craft, and did not show a single steamboat, though thirteen years had passed since Robert Fulton's genius had caused the Clermont to puff her triumphant way from New York to Albany in thirty-two hours, and now there were lines running between this and other ports in half the time. On Mark's right towered a structure which has since been dwarfed into Castle Garden, but was then Fort Clinton, a grim redoubt, with black muzzles of cannon peering seaward through embrasures eight feet thick.

Soon a pang of pity assailed Mark. He veered round, changing his view of the merry and scintillant waters for one of bowery and path-woven arcades. Just then he saw Gerald approaching him. Without a word spoken by either, the two friends linked arms and walked along the main marine promenade for some time in complete silence, bowing now and then to acquaintances of either sex; for this was the fashionable hour of strollers on the Battery, and one bowed, if one had the privilege of knowing them, to Beekmans, Livingstons, De Peysters, and other scions of aristocracy in a town which numbered only a hundred thousand inhabitants at the most.

Presently conversation was resumed between the young men. Mark spoke cheeringly of the chances in favor of Pamela Verplanck's recovery, scoffed the idea of her illness having the sentimental origin assigned it, and counselled Gerald, with earnest warmth, to hope that the future would smile on his present despairing suit.

That evening he was expected to sup with the Verplancks at seven o'clock. He went to their house in a mood of unwonted depression. It had deeply wounded him to learn that so silly and unfounded a tale had got wind concerning poor sick Pamela and himself. The thought that it might have reached Charlotte's ears, or those of her father, filled him, too, with embarrassing dread.

Charlotte soon came fluttering to meet him, in the prim, formal, colonial-looking parlor, with its spider-legged hair-cloth furniture and its massive mahogany doors.

He kissed her on one blooming cheek, but she darted coyly backward before he could kiss the other.

"You're late, sir," she said. "Supper's on the table, and father and Pamela and I had almost given you up. Dinah's a tyrant, you know, and always makes deliberate failures of both her muffins and corn-cakes when she's asked to postpone them a single minute. Father's said 'grace'; and, oh, I forgot—Colonel Burr is supping with us this evening, too."

"Colonel Burr?" repeated Mark, remembering his recent little panegyric of that celebrity. "And Charlotte," he went on, "pray tell me: how is your sister?"

"A little brighter since morning, I think."

"That's good news."

"She came down to supper, though somewhat too feeble. I believe, really, Mark, that she only came because of you."

"Because of me? Nonsense!"

"Why, how uncivilly you say that. Are you sorry poor Pamela should be glad to have you come?"

"Sorry? I? How absurd, Charlotte! Shall we go down, then?"

The dining-room was in the basement, only a few steps from the kitchen. As she returned thither, Charlotte took her vacated place at the head of the table, before two high silver kettles, one for tea, one for coffee. A turbaned negress was in waiting, with a dish of smoking corn-cakes. Except a plate or two of cooling muffins, this was the only warm viand. For the rest, there was cold sliced meat, marmalade in low heavy cut-glass bowls, and a large decanter of whiskey.

"No stimulant, thank you, sir," Colonel Burr was saying, while Mark approached him with outstretched hand. He was waving away the proffered decanter with his own slim white hand, but he instantly reversed it in Mark's direction, and gave to the young man a most cordial greeting. Already the belated guest had spoken a word of welcome and apology to both Pamela and her father.

"How horribly ill Pamela is looking!" Mark thought, as he seated himself.

"Colonel," said Varick Verplanck, pouring some syrup on a corn-cake which he had already carefully buttered, "I have rarely, if ever, known so abstemious a military man as yourself. Indeed, if you will allow me to say so, it has for years been my experience that all soldiers are rather liberal drinkers."

Aaron Burr laughed, crumbling a bit of bread between his shapely, womanish fingers. "Oh, sir," he replied, "I'm no longer a soldier. I'm only a poor struggling lawyer in a great city, nine-tenths of whose inhabitants think me the most evil of reprobates."

Charlotte was just then re-filling with coffee the speaker's third cup. "Colonel Burr," she exclaimed, with her bare arm curved over the shining implement in a way that Mark silently adored, "you are the last of men, I should say, to disdain the dignity of being a soldier. Only the other day somebody had the impudence to tell me that you had played but a minor part at the siege of Quebec in 1775. I wouldn't have that for a moment. I stood up for you with great valiance, feeling thrice-armed because my quarrel was just."

"Dear young lady," said Burr, his mobile face mellowing into an instant smile, "you make me feel recompensed for one of the hardest campaigns in all my military career."

"Pardon me, colonel," said Verplanck, with a stately little bow. "Our good and great Washington did that in the succeeding year, half by raising your rank and half by seeking you as his guest at Richmond Hill."

"Ah, sir," sighed Burr, slowly stirring the coffee which had now reached him, "Washington labored under the disadvantage of not being one of the most charming young women I have ever known, and also of serving his friends with very indifferent coffee—by no means the ambrosial beverage which your gifted daughter has the magic art of brewing."

"A very happy compliment, sir," laughed Mark Frankland, "but we all suspect, I fear, that it is paid Miss Charlotte for the modest purpose of turning conversation away from your brilliant exploits at Quebec."

"True, indeed!" cried Charlotte. "I insisted that as the aide-de-camp of General Arnold you not only fought with fine bravery, but endured the severest privations in that arduous winter march."

"Still more might be told," here struck in Pamela, who was trifling with her food rather than eating it, and whose glance kept haunting Mark's face in a way that he would probably not have observed but for his late converse with Gerald. "When General Montgomery met his heroic death," the girl continued, "there among those masses of ice on the borders of St. Lawrence, Colonel Burr—or Major Burr, as he was then called—caught the body of the fallen patriot and bore it to shelter within his own lines, amid a shower of bullets from the British troops."

"Brava, Pamela!" exclaimed Charlotte, waving a teaspoon in applausive mock frenzy. "But why, dear sister, did you not address Colonel Burr while you recalled in such neat phrase his glorious act of courage?"

The invalid turned suddenly toward Charlotte with a wild look of irritation and challenge.

"What do you mean?" she asked.

"Why, only this, dear Pamela: all the time you spoke you were looking straight at Mark Frankland, yonder, as though he and not Colonel Burr were the author of this handsome historic deed."

"I—I didn't know . . I—I didn't intend," stammered Pamela. The next moment, with twitching features, she rose from the table, in evident disarray. As she hurried toward the door, Charlotte followed her. Both girls disappeared, and soon a sound of sobs broke from the outer hall, promptly growing fainter as if through increased distance.

Mr. Verplanck looked almost pitiably embarrassed, and presently said, with apologetic suavity, to Burr,—

"My poor child's health is wretchedly broken. Pray forgive her curious outburst of sensitiveness. It comes merely from shattered nerves, poor Pamela, and is quite foreign to her gentle and kindly nature."

"As if I did not know that, my dear Verplanck!" hastened Burr, with the richest show of sympathy. He went on speaking, in his fluent and cordial way; but meanwhile Verplanck's look had transferred itself to Mark, who almost guiltily lowered his own.

Burr left unusually early, that evening, being called away, as he stated, by the necessity of preparing a brief in an imminent and urgent law-case. Verplanck went with him to the front door up-stairs, and then rejoined Mark in the basement dining-room.

"That man is a wonder," Verplanck said, after the little silence that ensued upon his return. "Can I help you to anything more, Frankland?"

"Nothing more, sir," said Mark, and added, in the polite idiom of the time, "I have had a great plenty, thank you—have supped most heartily on your excellent victuals."

"As I was saying," Verplanck resumed, "Colonel Burr is a wonder. There in his office just off Broadway in Reade Street, he goes on practising law and actually succeeding, in the teeth of enormous debt and a national unpopularity which is inveterate."

Here Verplanck rose again, and brought his chair to within a few inches of Mark's. He had a fine, cameo-like face, to which his high stock lent distinction. He laid one hand on Mark's shoulder for a moment, saying quickly and with graver voice,—

"But I did not mean, now that we are alone together, to mention so threadbare a topic as that of poor Aaron Burr's complete social downfall, or his remarkable struggle against tides of disaster. The truth is, Frankland, I was rather glad he made so early a departure."

"Glad, Mr. Verplanck?"

"Yes. It gives me a chance to speak with frankness on a subject very painful, and yet commandingly important. A subject, Frankland, that concerns my daughter."

"Miss Charlotte?" said Mark, with a speed almost tumultuous.

"No—not Charlotte. . . You and I have spoken of *her* not long ago, in privacy like this, have we not?"

"Indeed, yes," replied· Mark, flushing, and with a fiery sweetness in tone and look. "You have sanctioned my addresses, dear sir, and I am waiting—with only too much eagerness—the time when you will permit them to be made public."

"It is not of Charlotte that I wish to speak, but of Pamela," slowly said Verplanck.

Mark furtively gnawed his lips. "Poor Miss Pamela seems to be very sick."

"She *is* very sick." Envisaging Mark suddenly with his kind, faded, sorrowful eyes, Verplanck went on: "Yesterday Dr. Wainwright gave me his final word. Our dear Pamela is doomed. It is atrophy of the heart; the end has become certain. My poor darling is wasting away just as her mother did, twelve years ago. I myself recognize the symptoms. Her mother was much older than Pamela when *she* went, it is true. But I can see the same forlorn change, made all the more evident because of an intense maternal resemblance."

"Yes, yes," murmured Mark, aimlessly, and without even the interrogative note in his voice. He was pierced by a peculiar dread, which he could not explain and could only feel.

"There is no chance," pursued Verplanck, "of saving my child's life. But there is a chance of making her very happy during the few months which now remain to her. Charlotte has lately suspected this chance. To me its cheering possibility has become certain. Mark Frankland, my youngest daughter has fallen in love with you. She is passionately attached to you. It is a violent and absorbing infatuation."

Verplanck quitted his chair, and walked away, with bowed head. Mark sat quite still for a slight while. Then he abruptly rose and met the elder man as he turned and faced him in the mellow candle-light.

"You tell me this, sir," he said, with agitation, "and I perceive that the telling of it costs you deep regret."

"Regret and humiliation both!"

"And your telling it at all," pursued Mark, "shows the intensity of your conviction. Still, you may be wrong. If you are——"

"I am not wrong. The thing is

beyond doubt." Here Verplanck for a moment shrouded his face in a kerchief, dashing it hastily across his eyes as he again looked full at Mark. "Listen, my boy: Pamela has herself confessed to me this infatuation. In a way, being the younger, she is my favorite, though God knows I love each daughter with deepest affection! I would take in Charlotte's case no other course than I am taking in hers. Yes, she has told me, though in the most sacred secrecy. I violate my promise to her, and in doing so I firmly believe, Frankland, that I am telling the first actual lie of my whole life. Yet it is a lie told in the passionate fatherly hope of easing her final hours on earth. We will soon go into the country, as you know. She loves the old farm at Throgg's Neck, so replete for her with childish memories. Change of scene, partial change of air, may cause her to rally a little and seemingly improve. But, as I have said, the end is both sure and near. She cannot last through the summer. Yesterday she was so weak for hours that she could scarcely lift a hand. Then youth and native vitality conquered again, and to-day she has been better. Your expected coming, Frankland, had much to do with this altered state. Charlotte's thoughtless words, entirely innocent, caused the nervous shock that you saw. And yet, as I said, Charlotte is not ignorant of the truth. And, more than this (as .. as I think I before hinted), she is willing to join with me in the request I am now about to make."

There was silence, and Mark

looked wonderingly at the pale, distressed face before him.

"What request?" he asked.

"This, Frankland, this.".. And then Verplanck, with eager, plaintive volubility, spoke on for several seconds.

Mark sprang up from the table, shocked, with darkening brows.

"Oh, no, no!" he exclaimed, "not that! Of all things, not that! Believe me, sir, I could not possibly consent!"

III.

AT this same moment, after hearing every word that Mark had just spoken, Charlotte slipped into the room. She divined swiftly the motive of her lover's flurried speech. She went up to Verplanck's side and said, confronting Mark, with a hand thrown suddenly about her father's neck,—

"I know what it is to which you will not consent. But pray let me join my entreaty with father's!"

"It would be hypocrisy," shuddered the young man.

"Hypocrisy," Charlotte urged, "in a merciful cause!"

"It would ease that poor child's last hours," pleaded Verplanck, "far beyond any comfort that could reach her."

"And no one but we three," persisted Charlotte, "would ever know the truth."

"The truth!" Mark echoed, forlornly. "Call it, rather, the falsehood!"

Charlotte's face hardened a little. "It would be justifiable," she said. "You could do it for my sake, if you chose, as a sacrifice."

"I would make, for you," protested Mark, "almost any sacrifice."

"Make this, then," said Verplanck, with melancholy sternness.

"Make this, then," said Charlotte, echoing her father with tender emphasis.

"Soil my honor," faltered Mark, half as if to his own thoughts, "by asking a woman to be my wife whom I do not love and whom I have no intention of marrying?"

"Ah, if you put it that way!" sighed Verplanck.

"And you *need* not put it that way," fervidly supplemented Charlotte. "Tell yourself, instead, that you would be acting a merciful part to a dying girl!"

Mark moved away. Verplanck's eyes and those of his daughter followed him as he passed, with lowered head, to the opposite end of the room. Abruptly he paused, turned, and then said,—

"Pamela has always been capricious since a little girl. You both know how many were her whims and how quickly they would alter. I think you both exaggerate, in your love and pity for her, this new fancy. Not long ago she was all smiles to poor Gerald Suydam. Suddenly she chose to treat him with great coolness. The year before last, if I err not, she would scarcely notice Colonel Burr; now, as we have lately witnessed, she cannot hold him in too high esteem. I—I feel confident," finished Mark, dashing out these latter words with impetuous force, "that this is a mere mood, and will vanish as quickly as it came."

"It will only vanish with her death," sighed Verplanck.

Charlotte looked at Mark with every sign of its old sweetness gone from her face.

"Very well, then," she said. "If you think like this you cannot be persuaded,—that is all."

"Yes," Verplanck sighed, "that *is* all." He went up to Mark and held out his hand. He was very pale, and the hand that Mark took felt strangely cold. "I don't deny what you've just said, Frankland, my boy. She's been a perfect will-o'-the-wisp for changeability, whimsicality, ever since she was five years old——"

"No, father——"

"Yes, Charlotte, it's true. And what we ask is not merely difficult —it's ridiculous. Now that he refuses, as I suppose any sensible man would, I begin to see its entire absurdity." He gave a wistful, apologetic glance at Mark. "Good-night. Pardon a father who spoke far more from his paternal fondness, anxiety, sense of coming bereavement, than from the rational stand-point of which you have reminded him." And before Mark could find even a fragmentary sentence of response, Verplanck had quitted the room.

Charlotte, however, remained, and hardly ten minutes had elapsed when Mark was informing her that she deported herself like the most unfeeling termagant.

Then their first real quarrel occurred. "Very well," said Charlotte; "termagants oughtn't to marry."

Mark burst into a laugh. "Oh, Charlotte! Was there ever such a situation? You threaten to break our troth because I will not make love to another woman!"

"You must not speak like that," fumed Charlotte, "of my poor, dying sister! It's—it's—grossly disrespectful."

"*How* is it, in the name of common sense? To call her another woman? Certainly she isn't another man."

"Now you're horribly flippant—and cruel, besides!"

"Charlotte, my *dear* girl, *do* be sensible!"

"I'm human—if that's what you mean by *not* being sensible."

"It strikes me that you're *in*-human, toward myself."

"I'm not speaking of you or thinking of you. I'm speaking and thinking of poor, dear Pamela."

"But you're asking me to behave like the most insincere of mortals."

"Oh, yes, I know. You can phrase it that way, if you please."

"Phrase it that way! But I don't want to conduct myself that way."

"You ought to want to—under the circumstances. All men can, if they choose."

"What a magnificent revelation of your faith in our sex! So we're all rascals at heart, are we? I'm glad to learn you have so lofty an opinion of us."

Charlotte began to weep. "The more I see of your sex," she quavered, "the loftier seem your opinions of yourselves."

Her tears troubled Mark very much. They troubled him more as they continued to flow. He went near to her and touched one of her firm, ivory wrists, and told her that it broke his heart to see her weep. She at once put the wrist behind her back, and receded a little, and answered to the effect that his heart was an organ whose brittleness he entirely misrepresented. He endeavored to argue this point with her, mildly and very miserably, and at last, with a volcanic desperation, exclaimed,—

"Oh, very well! I'll be goose enough, traitor enough, to attempt this idiotic masquerade! But heaven help me to carry it through in any other than the most bungling fashion! Oh, I promise you I'll cut a pretty figure! And pray how will *you* like it if you see me hugging Pamela with all my might, and swearing to her eternal devotion?"

"Pamela," frowned Charlotte, "is far too much of an invalid to be *hugged!* You must behave very carefully. You must recollect the delicate state of her health."

"How delightful!" he groaned. "Go on, please, with your instructions."

She fluttered to him, and, with the nodding head-movement of a bird, kissed him lightly and swiftly on either cheek.

"I knew you'd consent!" Her own cheeks were roses, her eyes were liquid stars. "Now you're my own dear Mark again!"

"I beg your pardon," he objected,

with sarcastic calm; "I've become Pamela's dear Mark."

He slept very ill that night, and informed his father, the next day, that he felt too unwell to appear at the "store." His father, who had been often accused by strait-laced acquaintances of indulging him foolishly, at once grew worried and advised his son by all means to leave ledgers and accounts alone and get as many hours as he could in the open air.

"It's a fine day, Mark," said Ezra Frankland, "finer than yesterday." The old merchant had lost three children before their mother died. Mark, the last left, was the apple of his eye. "You might go up in the country—say as far as the canal. It's pleasant and shady up there, by this time. You could drop in at your aunt Elizabeth's place and get dinner. She'd be mighty glad to see you."

The "canal" was where Canal Street now roars with traffic. It had been, until 1809, or thereabouts, the famed Collect Pond, a picturesque resort of boating parties in summer and skaters in winter. It was now transformed into a broad canal, with paved streets and lines of trees on either side. Mark might easily have gone thither by stage-coach, but he preferred to avoid a haunt consecrated, in former times, by many happy strolls with Charlotte.

The thing that he had consented to do filled him with sorrowful dismay. His honest nature revolted from it; the thought of its odious coming experience darkened the blue May sky over Bowling Green, and gave to the familiar dormer-windowed brick houses along Broadway a dreary, alien look.

He loitered up past Trinity Church, at whose doors, not many years before, Gouverneur Morris had delivered to an immense concourse his impassioned funeral eulogy over the bier of Hamilton. Prim, colonial, and in spots village-like, the town gave no prophecy of those prodigious changes which awaited it. How Mark would have marvelled and thrilled if for a few instants all should have been fore-shadowed to him as the future destined it,—a monstrous post-office looming from the placid lower angle of City Hall Park; huge sky-scraping structures upheaving themselves in Printing House Square; legions of massive edifices shutting out all view of either Hudson or East River; Wall Street growing in a trice from drowsy quietude to bustle and tumult; the hubbub of countless vehicles deafening one's ears; the clangor of the cable cars blending with thunders from elevated trains; the wider thoroughfares vying in their streams of pedestrianism with the peaceful side-streets; and human life everywhere intensifying itself, materializing itself, making itself an imperious, vivid, unavoidable dominance!

In his perplexity and depression he somehow thought of Aaron Burr, and soon drifted into a little dingy pair of rooms on Reade Street, not far from where the old white marble Stewart building now stands. Mark was always sure of a glad welcome when he crossed the threshold of this office, which thousands of his countrymen would have deemed their feet soiled by touching.

Burr, seated before a broad table loaded with papers and books, rose and cordially clasped the hand of his young friend. The next moment he turned toward a man who had been stationed at his elbow as Mark appeared. The man's attire was not of the choicest, but he had an honest, intelligent look.

"This bill, colonel, has been running a good while."

Burr laid a hand on his arm. "I know it, my good fellow," he answered, with a faint shrug and the most sympathetic of smiles. "But, alas! the well is dry to-day." Here he pointed to a square hole made of piled books in the centre of the table, and then suddenly dove a searching hand into its hollow.

"Bless my soul!—not a dollar left! I don't see how my well got so dry as soon as this. I received quite a sum of money two or three days ago. But people came to me with all sorts of piteous stories. Those are nearly the only kinds of people, except my few clients, who *do* come nowadays. And I must have . . er . . miscalculated the amount of . . er . . *water* that my poor little well contained."

" I should very much like to have the money this morning, colonel," persisted the man, in a voice urgent yet low.

" So sorry . . so sorry, my friend! Come again in a few days. There's no telling but what you may find me a perfect Crœsus then. No telling, I assure you."

A few more words were interchanged between debtor and creditor before the latter at length reluctantly took his leave.

Burr turned, with his most charming smile, to Mark. "You know about my well, don't you?" he said, motioning for his guest to be seated.

"Yes," smiled Mark; "you've told me about it. Ah, colonel, if you'll let me say so, it's strange that a man of your great powers should be such a child in money matters!"

"You may say to me anything you please, my dear Mark. You may scold me as much as you like. By the Eternal, as my stanch old friend Andrew Jackson is wont to swear, I deserve a sound flogging very often for my improvidence!"

"Your well, as you name it, colonel, has no doubt been dried up by charities. You're the most charitable man I've ever known."

"Yes, my boy—immorally so.

I give what belongs to others!"
Here Burr sighed; then, with return
of the brisk sparkle which had briefly
left his dark blue eyes,—

"Pray, to what do I owe the
honor of this visit? You look
troubled. Gad, I hope you've got
into some scrape that I can legally
pull you out of! I like dealing with
you sons of rich merchants." And
here he laughed his mellow, con-
tagious laugh. "You're sheep, sir,
worth the pleasure of shearing."

"I haven't got into any scrape of
that sort, colonel."

"Then it's a woman—I'll be
bound it's a woman, you sly young
blade!" And Burr gave his visitor
a sharp slap on the thigh. "If so,
Mark, you're devilish sensible to
come to an old veteran sinner like
me."

"Don't paint yourself in black

colors, colonel. I won't have you
do so even in jest. . . Yes," added
Mark, with a solemn little nod, "it
is a woman." And then he told
something that made his listener's
fine face both pale and darken.

"How extraordinary!" burst from
Burr, when he had ended.

"You—you think, sir, I am wrong
in having consented?"

"Wrong? In the name of decent
compassion, no! Poor Verplanck!
poor Charlotte! and ah, poor Pamela! What a situation! Zounds!
somebody ought to put it on the
stage and play it over at the Park
Theatre! Ah, no, no—I don't mean
that, my boy—I don't mean anything so heartless!" Tears stood
in the speaker's eyes—those eyes
which had blazed in battle, which
had helped the oratoric art of their
possessor to electrify listening

senates. "Bravo, my dear Mark! Your resolve has just the right note in it—a note of chivalry all the surer because so difficult, so unusual, so austere! I don't wonder you found it hard to consent. Pamela's a chameleon, as you've just hinted. But all her volatile, mutable frivolity becomes sanctified, now, by the nearness of death. Good God! what a love-test! But you'll stand it—you'll carry it to a mournfully triumphant end. I, for one, trust you. And as for blessing you, I leave that to her father and sister—especially the last! Don't waver in the least. I've seen life; I know women. And, believe me, Charlotte will love you all the better in years to come for having served her with so splendid a loyalty!"

IV.

AARON BURR'S encomium and encouragement dwelt stimulatingly with Mark for a good while after he had gone forth again into the glad spring weather from those dismal and almost poverty-stricken little chambers fronting the old City Hall. His nerves were still in a state of marked disquiet, however, since the ordeal of his coming dissimulation was to begin that same afternoon. He stopped at a tobacconist's shop below the American Museum on the corner of Ann Street, and bought a few cigars of fairly good quality—the best which he could procure—at four cents apiece. He lit one of them, and stood looking up abstractedly at the impossible animals painted on wooden ovals and dotting the entire façade of the spacious building.

"Oh, it's you, Mark?" said a voice; and, turning, he beheld Gerald Suydam.

"Good-morning," replied Mark. "You're at leisure, like me?"

"No, indeed," returned Gerald, as they walked southward in mutually accepted company. "Father sent me up to Pearl Street about a bill of lading. He's a good deal stricter with me, as you know, than yours is with you. He says he was brought up not to shirk business, or Suydam, Van Horn & Co. wouldn't be the merchants they are to-day. I suppose he's right. But I often wish he were as lax and complaisant as *your* father is."

"Oh, dad knows how to scold, sometimes."

Gerald laughed. "I wonder what mine would say if he saw me smoking a cigar in the street. . . And, by the bye, Mark, isn't it a little daring of you?"

"Daring? Humbug!"

"Well, you know," demurred Gerald, with an assertive head-toss, "folks will talk."

"Oh, I know, yes."

"Three-quarters of your male acquaintance, in your own rank of life, think that for a man of your age to smoke a cigar during business hours is an act of gross dissipation. Here comes old Mr. Ludlow Vanderveer. I can see the look of horror gathering on his puckered little face."

"I shall pretend I don't see it," said Mark, a trifle sullenly—"or its owner, either." After moving on a few more yards, however, he threw away his cigar. "The fact is, Gerald," he continued, "I'm a good deal upset; I feel like having something to soothe me—and I don't take big sly draughts of Jamaica rum, as they say Mr. Ludlow Vanderveer does. A rather nasty thing has happened to me since I saw you yesterday, Gerald. It concerns our recent talk, too. I don't know that I ought to tell it you. I—I meant to tell scarcely a soul. But I'll let you know it if you give me your solemn oath that you'll keep it the deadest of secrets."

With curiosity instantly roused, Gerald hesitated, nevertheless, to engage in so momentous a compact. He was excessively conscientious, and had a strong streak of piety besides; he had once seriously thought of studying for the ministry.

"Oh, very well," said Mark, with pitiless disregard of his reluctance, "perhaps it's better I did *not* tell you. After all, it might only make you unhappy."

This was too much for Gerald, and he soon agreed to face the full profanity of the "solemn oath." When he had made complete acquiescence, Mark divulged his important tidings.

The recital caused Gerald to turn pale as paper. "You're shocked," said Mark, watching him.

"I'm horrified," came the gasped answer.

"You think me wrong, then, to have consented?"

"Unspeakably wrong!"

For a moment Mark forgot himself.

"I've just been talking it all over with an older and much wiser man than you are. Colonel Burr thinks the act heroic in its mercy."

"Aaron Burr may think so!" exclaimed Gerald, with haughty intolerance. "And I dare say he *is* much *wiser* than I am. But, oh, Mark!" and here the young man's voice for a moment failed him, "why—why did you tell it me at all? The girl I love! you know how dearly I have loved her, and love her still! And to dream of deceiving her so terribly! It's ghastly —it's unpardonable. The fact that she is dying makes it all the more so... Mark, Mark, I—I am ashamed of you!"

And with glittering eyes and steps that reeled unsteadily, Gerald hurried from his friend, who stood staring after him, half in anger, half in self-reproach.

V.

"I DON'T want to go into the country at all this summer!" exclaimed Pamela Verplanck, a few days later, to her sister Charlotte. "It will be such a long, horrid journey for *him* to take every day from the city by stagecoach."

"Couldn't you get along," asked Charlotte, "with his coming three times a week?"

"No. I *must* see him every day. I'll speak to father about our not leaving. He'll consent; he does anything I ask, now I'm so sick." Here Pamela leaned forward in her easy-chair and took a little hand-mirror from a side table. "Charlotte," she presently said.

"Well, Pamela."

"Don't you think I look rather better than I did?" She turned away from the mirror and almost avidly scanned Charlotte's fair and healthful face with her own haggard, glassy eyes.

Charlotte was sewing industriously at some useful fabric. Like nearly all the ladies of her land and time, young or old, she rarely plied her needle, except in company, at lighter decorative tasks.

"Yes," she said, not meaning a word, "you do look better, I think." Then she added, very sweetly, "And you feel stronger, do you not?"

"I feel happier, and there's so much in that! It has been such a strange, delicious surprise to me, this realization that Mark wants me for his wife! And to think, Charlotte, how I always suspected—

always *believed*, in fact—that he preferred *you!* I asked him about this yesterday."

"Did you?" said Charlotte, stitching away.

"Yes; and he laughed, and answered—what do you think he answered?"

"I'm sure I don't know, Pamela dear."

"Perhaps I shouldn't tell you; it may annoy you. But never mind; you're not sick like me; you won't bother about it."

"Tell me what Mark said," Charlotte gently urged. She had let her work fall unheeded in her lap.

"He said," hesitated Pamela, "that . . that—well, Charlotte, that he had always somehow felt you were cut out for an old maid."

Charlotte's needle was now making quick, diligent plunges. She had lowered her face a little, perhaps to hide its insurgent wave of color.

That evening she met Mark soon after he arrived. "How is your sister?" he at once asked.

"Her spirits are greatly improved."

"Your own do not seem exactly buoyant."

Charlotte gnawed, for a moment, her rosy underlip. "I don't think it quite good taste in you," she presently said, "to tell Pamela I was cut out for an old maid."

Mark started. "*Did* I tell her that? Oh, yes, I believe I did."

"You *believe* you did!" bristled Charlotte. "Of course you're very well aware that you did! And you might not have said anything quite so hateful about me."

"But I'm not inventive, Charlotte."

"It seems to me that you are, Mark—very!"

"I'm not used to this sort of dreadful deception. I naturally say the first thing (in the way of a falsehood) that comes into my head."

Charlotte looked unpacified. "You need not have uttered, then, quite so glaring a falsehood—that's all."

Mark smothered something decidedly like an oath. "I warned you that I'd make a botch of the whole abominable affair."

"Hush! She may be listening."

"I don't care if she is; I wish she were!" he growled, quite wildly.

"Mark!"

"Oh, you're not so haughty, now. I've frightened away your dudgeon, have I?"

Charlotte drew herself up. "I didn't think you could be so cowardly," she flung at him.

"No; neither did I. Nor so deceitful, either. And instead of getting encouragement from you, the arch-conspirator (for I'm certain you set your father up to this whole uncanny game), I receive reprimands and reproaches. It's too frightfully unjust. I can't endure it—I won't endure it—there!"

"Mark," implored Charlotte, "for *my* sake, persevere!" She was now all clemency and contrition. "Remember, it will be only for so short a time!"

"But you won't even let me kiss you while it continues!"

"No: that seems too much like hypocrisy."

"But, in the name of the Lord Almighty, what is it already?"

"Don't swear, Mark, please. It's a .. a splendid piece of self-sacrifice. Recollect how Colonel Burr regarded it."

"And how did Gerald Suydam regard it?"

"You should never have told him at all. I was thoroughly right in scolding you for doing so."

"Of course; you're always thoroughly right in scolding me," wailed Mark; "and you've done nothing else, whenever we've been alone together, since this hideous business began."

Charlotte benignly patted him on the shoulder. "I'll try to be more self-controlled in the future," she murmured. And then she opened the gates of heaven to him by giving him a smile that bathed all her face in tender glory and made her dimples glow for him like stars and rosebuds magically mixed. "There, now; be good and brave and noble. Go upstairs and see poor dear Pamela. In a little while supper will be ready. We're going to have waffles——"

"I detest waffles. They never agree with me."

"Then you needn't eat these. *I* mixed them, though, in the kitchen, with my own hands."

"Then I'll devour twenty!" He tried to slip an arm about her waist, but she darted backward and raised a monitory finger. . .

May ended, that year, with a few days of our proverbial New York heat, but June proved delightfully salubrious. Dr. Wainwright scowled a little when Mr. Verplanck informed him that his invalid daughter was obstinately adverse to leaving town. Then, after a

A Romance of

slight interval of seeming medita-
tion, the doctor suddenly shrugged
his shoulders and said, with crisp
brevity,—

"Oh, very well. Let her have
her own way."

"Poor child!" lamented Verplanck. "You mean, of course,
doctor, that the end is so near——"

"No," interrupted the other, with
sharp, unexpected dissent, "I don't
mean anything of the sort." Then
he spoke a few more words that
caused his hearer's face to light up
with eager gladness.

"Why, doctor, you can't possibly
imply . . ?"

"It's no implication, Mr. Verplanck," was the rather stiff retort.
"It's an assertion, as far as it goes,
and you may take it for what it's
worth."

"But," almost panted Verplanck,

78

"it seems to go very far and to be worth a great deal."

"Your daughter, sir, has decidedly improved. That is all I dare to state at present."

"But you stated (and Dr. Wilton, in consultation with you, also stated) that my darling's heart was fatally diseased."

"*I* never stated it, sir. Wilton did, I think. But please don't tell Wilton either that I stated he stated it or that I myself didn't state it." Here Dr. Wainwright, who had a large good-humored mouth, closed his lips in morose compression. The next moment he grumblingly pursued, "Wilton and I have known one another forty years, and we're the best of friends. But we average one severe professional quarrel every six months. There's no use in adding to the number." And very soon afterward Dr. Wainwright took his leave.

Verplanck was so thrilled with happy hope that for several hours he went about his various duties in a kind of delicious daze. From this pleasant condition Charlotte rudely roused him, however, by the tidings that Pamela had had another of her weak seizures while Mark was reading aloud to her from Moore's "Lalla Rookh"—a work then in great vogue among sweethearts of both the "mother country" and our own.

VI.

BUT Pamela's illness proved transient. The next day she was decidedly better, and remained thus all through the following week, during which the thermometer stood so high that it filled Vauxhall Garden, up town between Broadway and the Bowery and partly on the site of the present Astor Library, with citizens who came to take cooling drinks there and hear the playing of the band.

"I really think," said Mark to Charlotte, one day, "that you ought to use your influence with her on the subject of going to Throgg's Neck."

"I haven't any influence," replied Charlotte. "Nobody has, nowadays, except you."

Mark suppressed a groan, "But it would let me 'off duty' a little."

"Do you find your 'duty' so tedious?"

"You know very well that I wouldn't endure doing it at all but for these occasional stolen interviews with you."

"At Throgg's Neck," said Charlotte, with maddening sedateness, "you wouldn't see me half as often as you see me now."

"True," he blustered, "but how *do* I see you now? As if I were a prisoner up at the jail near Chatham Row, and you were allowed sometimes to dawn on me before the gratings of my cell. . . By the way, it strikes me that Pamela is wonderfully stronger and better."

"Yes, Mark. Isn't it charming to see the change?"

"Charming? Oh, yes—of course

it's charming. But then, don't you know, we . . we didn't expect her to recuperate like this."

"Recuperate! What a curious word!"

"It's a perfectly good English word."

"I didn't say it wasn't," retorted Charlotte, with sternness. "But, for all that, it has such a large, heartless, lawyer-like sound. I may be unreasonable, of course."

"It strikes me that you're thoroughly unreasonable."

The next fortnight was a crucial one for Mark. Pamela, when weak and languid, was often a petulant and exacting mistress. But now, when each day seemed to lend her fresh vitality, she became almost tyrannically wilful.

"I like you to give me my medicine," she would say to Mark, "and yet you always manage to arrive just after I have taken it." Or again, " I send both Charlotte and father out of the room, so that we can be alone together (as two lovers ought to be, at least once a day), and you sit staring at me in the oddest silence. You make me do all the talking."

"You talk so well," said Mark, veiling his misery behind a smile.

"And then there's another point: you're not half so much overjoyed at my recovery as father and Charlotte seem to be. Why, pray, is this ?"

"Oh, Pamela," said Mark, with an acute conscience-pang, "you surely can't think I am not pleased to have you get well!"

"Pleased?" And she rapped him on the ear somewhat sharply with the fan that had lain in her lap. "I should think, sir, you might choose some warmer word."

"I—I meant it to be warm, Pamela, but I have not your expressive gifts of language."

"Oh, you haven't?" she mocked. "It seems to me that in former days I have heard you employ a good deal of both fluency and eloquence when the mood stirred you."

On the following afternoon he found her dressed in bonnet and mantilla and waiting for him in the parlor.

"I've been feeling so well today," she announced, "that I asked Dr. Wainwright if I could not go out. He has consented, but restricts me to a stroll of only three times round Bowling Green."

Charlotte and her father now entered the room. Mark wondered, as he greeted them, whether they observed how pale he had grown.

"It will be my first appearance out of doors since our engagement," continued Pamela, with a few dainty touches at her long plum-colored mitts. "Of course, as it hasn't been made publicly known yet, I suppose I oughtn't to take your arm. Still," she added, with a gay flirt of her pretty frilled gown, "I believe I will, after all. People can say what they please. Besides, very few that we care about may see us; so many of them have gone into the country."

Mark caught Charlotte's eye. She dropped her look and turned away, trying to smile; he saw how painful a failure she made of the effort. Then he glanced at Varick Verplanck. The latter gave a twist to his stock with both hands, and then coughed nervously.

"Wait supper for us," called out Pamela, merrily, as she went into the hall. "I expect to have quite an appetite when I return."

Their walk, three times round Bowling Green, was torture to Mark. The heat had relented of late; it was a perfect midsummer evening. Flashes from the Bay came to them between the tossing trees of the Battery. The sun, setting in great splendor, as though far out at sea, shot bars of dusty gold over the railed enclosure of the Green, gilding its clustered lilac-bushes. Overhead some gauzy clouds had grown a spectral pink. Pamela had taken Mark's arm, and she leaned upon it with a jauntily confidential air. Her face, below its big white-feathered bonnet of straw, gleamed

with distinct semblance of its former prettiness; rose-tints like reflections from the sky touched it,
and a new, clear sparkle, as of
restored health, radiated from the
gaze which she turned, at brief
intervals, toward her companion.

They met few people, and none
whom they chanced to know. Pamela laughed and chatted with
spirited volubility.

"Do you know, Mark, I feel able
to walk ten times the distance pre-
scribed by Dr. Wainwright? Isn't
it a lovely evening? I suppose that
if anybody should see us walking
arm in arm like this the inference
would merely be that you'd taken
me out for an invalid's airing, as an
old friend of the family. . . And
by the way, Mark, do you know
that a very important matter occurred to me this morning? I con-

sider that you've been sadly remiss not to have thought of it. Perhaps you did think of it, however, and my illness prevented you from carrying it into effect. Can't you guess what I mean?"

"No, Pamela .. really .. I can't."

"My engagement ring, you know, Mark. I haven't yet received any."

"True. . . I—I will see to it at once."

When they paused at the stoop of her home Pamela declared that she was not in the least tired. During supper she insisted on eating one or two things that were forbidden to her, and even spoke of sitting up that evening a full hour beyond her accustomed time of retiring. On this plan, however, Verplanck laid an immediate veto; but it was nearly nine o'clock when she went upstairs at Charlotte's side.

The torment in Mark's soul at last found vent. He faced Verplanck there in the prim parlor, whose walls seemed to re-echo with Pamela's merry good-night and with her firmly declared resolve to enjoy a similar walk on the morrow —"only ever so much longer."

"Mr. Verplanck," he said, a little hoarsely, "you know that I love your daughter Charlotte."

"Yes, Mark, I know."

"And that I had asked you to let me marry her, and that you had promised me our engagement should transpire as soon as Charlotte completed her twenty-first year."

"Yes."

At this point Mark despairingly lifted both hands. "And now Pamela shows every sign of getting permanently well!"

"You are right," murmured Verplanck. "I—I spoke with Wainwright this afternoon. He has no longer the least doubt. My dear child is getting well with a most remarkable speed. It has all been, from the outset, a great medical mistake. Her trouble was nervous, not organic."

"Delightful tidings for *you*, sir. Delightful they would be for myself as well, were it not——Still, need I explain?"

"No—naturally."

"I granted your earnest request," Mark went on, with a dreary wildness. "Charlotte abetted you in this request. *Her* entreaties, I admit, were my chief cause of consent. But, now—what is to be done?"

Verplanck folded his arms and began to pace the floor, giving no answer except one or two perplexed shakings of his gray head.

"Up to the present time," proceeded Mark, "my position was defensible; I now feel that it is rapidly losing all excuse. You must agree with me, Mr. Verplanck, that the life-saving motive of my action will soon cease to exist."

"I can't deny this."

"And hence, sir, a single course will remain. Pamela, as soon as possible, must be told everything."

"As soon as possible," said a voice in the doorway. "But now is too early," Charlotte went on, with her face all anxiety, her tones all tremor. "Now it might kill her to be told!"

For a few seconds of silence these three people—alarmed, bewildered, distressed—stared into one another's faces.

Suddenly Mark gave a cry of bitter intolerance.

"I cannot go on like this," he said, seizing both of Charlotte's hands. "It will drive me crazy. The better she gets the harder I find it to play lover. To-day was an agony. To-morrow will be worse. Next day——Oh, I cannot, I can-*not!*"

VII.

CHARLOTTE forcibly withdrew her hands. A pained shine filled her humid eyes; the corners of her mouth were trembling.

"If you want to kill my poor sister," she said, "you will shatter this new happiness. All we now ask is that you shall wait. . . Is it not so?" And she turned with tragic appeal to her father.

"Yes," replied Verplanck, dismally. "That is all we ought to ask, beyond a doubt."

"If it were only that!" burst from Mark. "I'd *wait* willingly enough. But it's not merely waiting, at all; it's acting; it's getting every nerve of my body in a tingle; it's lying as

Old New York

I've never dreamed I *could* lie. Here is Pamela suddenly waking to the fact that I've given her no engagement ring. I've got to get her one to-morrow, I suppose. What a horrible mockery!"

Charlotte made toward him a quick, consoling movement. "Oh, never mind, Mark! It will do for *me* hereafter!"

He gave a harsh laugh. "Hereafter? A year from now? Or two? Or three?"

"Her convalescence," said Verplanck, with solemnity, biting his lips, "is—is extraordinarily swift. In a month she may be well enough to hear all."

"And denounce me as a villain."

"If she did that *now*," pleaded Charlotte, "it might kill her."

"I don't believe so," avowed Mark. "I don't believe my—my

95

mendacity has helped her recovery in the least. She has always been freakish, as you've both agreed. I chanced to become one of her freaks. She wasn't half as sick a girl as the doctors thought, or as either of you thought, and this physical betterment was bound, in any case, to come. She nearly broke poor Gerald Suydam's heart a year or two ago. Perhaps she wanted to try and break mine. But she will never succeed." He looked full at Charlotte. "It was broken before. You've got one piece, and I retain the other."

"Then I'll never give it back to you, so that you can mend the fragments and live a contented life," mournfully flashed Charlotte, "unless you stand firm for a while longer in this trying and most unforeseen difficulty."

"Oh, as you please!" cried Mark, while he walked toward the door with scowling face.

But here Verplanck hurried to Mark, and threw an arm detainingly, persuasively, round his neck. Charlotte's manner softened, a moment later. Then Mark, pierced with pity and feeling new throbs of love as he watched her worried face, felt also twinges of remorse. Perhaps all three were simultaneously beset by a sense of humor at the novel and totally unanticipated relations in which they stood. If so, all three realized, as well, the profanity of open laughter; and though many more words were spoken by each of them, Mark left the house, that evening, with his burden of bondage weightier than ever, and a full recognition of the wretchedly unsettled state in which all plaints and importunings had left his future.

Compassion, as he receded from the house, faded once more into qualms of self-injury. "What on earth am I going to do?" he inwardly moaned. "How on earth am I going to keep it up? The strain has already become unbearable!"

A yellow segment of moon was dropping low toward the west, flinging its glamorous light on the Brooklyn shore and making the dormer-windowed roofs of State Street darkly visible, as Mark drew near the house in which he lived. He had seen few passers, for the hour was a little beyond ten, and this meant, in the New York of that period, almost what midnight would mean now. Just as he had set his foot on the first step of his own stoop a figure came forward from the farther dimness.

"Gerald!"

"Yes, Mark; it's I. For over an hour I've waited in there with your father. But he grew drowsy, so I left, and have kept up a kind of sentinelship ever since."

"You wanted to see me, then?"

A closer view showed Mark how pale and drawn was Gerald's face.

"I *did* see you, Mark, this evening, just before twilight. I avoided you *both;* but I watched you."

"Well?"

"It was horrible! She leaned upon your arm; she looked up at you and smiled. She bore the signs of illness, but I could note that she was no longer feeble or sickly. Oh, Mark Frankland, I, who love that girl as dearly as I do, turned faint and giddy at the devilish sight!"

"Devilish, eh?" muttered Mark.

"Yes—there's no other word for it. You've bound me by an oath to secrecy, and it's an oath that my honor will not let me break. But when I think of the part you're enacting—when I think of the awful falsehood that you, who call yourself a gentleman, have been willing to live and persevere in for days past, then do I feel almost justified in scorning the promise I gave you, and publishing to society at large your shameless conduct!"

Mark's right foot had till now rested on the lowest step of the stoop. He drew it quickly back upon the sidewalk, and faced Gerald. He was very indignant. The mental irritation and turmoil of hours past seemed to centre in one choking ferment at his heart, and thence to send up in his brain a sort

of fiery mist. He was taller than
Gerald, and he now loomed above
his former friend with every feature
blent into one solid mask of wrath.
But he did not speak loudly; he
had the air of a man who disdains
explosiveness.

"You have insulted me grossly,
and you shall pay for it hereafter.
Only a friendship of so many years
could keep me from striking you
down like a vulgar ruffian—as you
know very well I have the power
to do. But for this jealous and
cowardly misvaluation of motives
honorable and disinterested, be sure
that you shall answer at some future time. I do not care to engage
now in a quarrel whose cause might
be guessed, and hence drag into
publicity a family I esteem. But
later I shall force you into either
facing me at the pistol's point or

amply retracting your insolence of to-night. Even to-morrow, if you please, however, you may send me your seconds, though it is in order that I, as the aggrieved party, should send you mine."

"I will meet you anywhere and at any time," replied Gerald, firmly. "I am not the coward you have called me. But I loathe duelling, and think it murder. And therefore I should fire in the air, though you might kill me if you chose."

These words were so characteristic of Gerald—so instinct with recollections to his hearer of a nature which he had long known as noble and brave, though deeply tinged with what he himself had often declared tiresome puritanism —that they wrought a speedy emotional change.

"Look here, Gerald," Mark said, with abrupt, gruff feeling, "you've just called me, in so many words, a brute. I answer that you're a fool. Shall it be quits between us? Quits, I mean, till either you apologize or I admit myself criminally sinful through seeking to save a fellow-creature's life."

Gerald had clutched the wooden railing of the court-yard near him. With bent head he answered,—

"I spoke rashly, madly—I grant it. But my love for that poor girl has almost crazed me." Here he raised his head, and the weird light made his features ghostly.

Mark sprang toward him, and put both arms about his form. There were tears in his eyes. Of old he had fought many a battle for Gerald, always weaker than he, always far more the student than the athlete.

A surge of boyish memories over-swept him now, as he gently shook Gerald's slenderer frame.

"You stupid fellow! Do you think I wouldn't go through fire-and-water to give you the girl you love if only I could? Do you dream I don't adore *Charlotte?* Do you fancy this thing isn't half killing *me* with vexation and botheration and in-fernal embarrassment? Do you suppose I ever expected it would grow into such a horrible mess and muddle? Do you suspect that Charlotte did, or that her father did? Do you imagine we're not, all three of us, half out of our wits with consternation and excitement?"

Their eyes met, quite close. "Mark," began the other, brokenly, "I'm sorry I . ."

"There . . there; that's enough." The sweat-drops were glistening on

Gerald's white face. Mark whipped out his handkerchief and mopped them off. " Go home and try to get some sleep. I'll see you, or write you, soon. God knows, if you don't sleep a wink you won't, I'll wager, be a whit worse off than this poor rival bugaboo into which you've absurdly magnified me !"

VIII.

"MY dear Mark," said Aaron Burr, the next morning, "it's all a very interesting and extraordinary case."

Mark, in his despair, had dropped into the grimy Reade Street rooms, and had made a clean breast there of all his troubles. Burr, who was the most brilliant talker in the town that prided itself on despising him, possessed also the tactful if less rare art of being a perfect listener. He now leaned back in his chair before the great flat desk so chaotically laden with papers and books, and musingly brushed against his chin the feathered end of an ink-stained quill.

"Colonel," suddenly exclaimed

Mark, after quite a long silence, "I feel that I am boring you. There were several people waiting to see you in the little hall outside before I came in, and I've been here an unconscionable time already."

Burr gave one of his gay, sweet laughs. "Thank God, they're not creditors this time, Mark! I've paid up all pressing debts for at least a fortnight. The fellows with mighty demands on me can't be among those you saw; they'd have pushed in without the least ceremony if they were. No, my boy, they're only beggars. They know the well isn't dry this morning. It's astonishing how the poor devils manage to *flairer* the repletion of that well! That's what comes of being a confirmed ass with one's money. They know I can't resist them when they begin their doleful tales. Old military comrades; old political supporters; new (but starving) sympathizers with me in my 'fallen greatness.' And some of them such delightful impostors! I'm afraid I too often reward the last merely for amusing me by their brazen impudence."

"Well, colonel," said Mark, drawing a deep breath as once again his host's full, sweet laugh rose and died away, "I'm a beggar, too, though merely for a few crumbs of wholesome counsel."

"Those I want to give you—those I will give you if I can," returned Burr, at once relapsing into his former serious pose. "Indeed, I would make them a whole loaf, were it only in my power. . . You tell me that a ship has just reached Boston, bringing your firm valuable goods, about whose custom-duties your father thinks there may be serious disagreements."

" Yes, colonel."

" And that he has just told you he deems it advisable for either him or yourself to make an immediate journey to Boston ?"

" Yes, colonel."

Burr continued to muse. The quill dropped unheeded from his fingers. Again and again he passed a hand slowly across his forehead. On a sudden he gave Mark one quick, imperative look.

" Go to Boston."

" You advise retreat, then ? You, a soldier ?"

" Go to Boston," Burr repeated, in much lower and more lingering voice. He seemed to address his own thoughts. He had changed his attitude once more. His clenched right hand, with its elbow resting on the front of the desk, was now supporting his slanted head. Watching his meditative face, full of shrewdness and power, Mark thought of how this man had escaped but by one or two votes being President of his country, and of how the brilliancy and audacity of his statesmanship had once made him the idol of that country as well.

"I have it," Burr said, at last, rising. "If there is any path out of the whole pathetic yet absurd tangle, I seem to have discerned one."

He now fixed upon Mark a look that brimmed both with sympathy and command. It amazed its recipient, because at once so tender and so austere. The next moment he quickly approached the young man, and sank into a chair at his side.

"I want to do you a service, my boy, and I think that I can. But you must throw yourself with a certain amount of blind confidence on my proffered assistance. You must not ask leading questions; you must permit yourself to regard me, Aaron Burr, as your good genius, and to envelop myself in a cloud of benevolent mysticism. I've always had a romantic streak in me, and I think that provided any future historian ever condescends to treat me at all he will be a very dull person if he does not perceive that my many faults and few virtues are all touched by the element of the picturesque. Surely" (with a sigh sweeping through these next words) "my misfortunes have been! Yes, everything said, I have succeeded picturesquely, I have failed picturesquely, I have starved picturesquely, and now (if it be not too bold self-flattery) I am travelling toward my allotted limit of three-score years and ten with a kind of dogged self-reliance that is nothing if not picturesque."

"True, colonel. I've no word of dissent."

Burr's hand clasped lightly his listener's arm. "So now I propose to solve this little social problem after my own picturesque pleasure. You must go to Boston, and you must remain there—if it be weeks and weeks—till I bid you return. Easy enough to write Pamela letters of excuse. Your detention is un-avoidable; a law-suit is threatened; it is all a matter involving thousands of dollars. As for your father, you must make him your willing abettor —not a hard task, since I well know that he adores you. There—these are my instructions. I will send you the formulas, now and then, of your various needful letters to Pamela; you will amplify them at your own discretion. As regards your real love-letters to ·Charlotte, those must always be addressed to me. I will see that they are safely delivered. Cupid himself could not serve you as a more efficient courier, and I—a sadly mature Cupid, it is conceded—will be far discreeter."

"Colonel," hesitated Mark, "I ____"

"One word more. This Mr. Gerald Suydam, who is so love-lorn and heart-stricken . . has Pamela ever given him any solid encouragement?"

"Yes—in the past."

"The past! You youngsters talking about a past! You mean that she threw him over a little while ago."

"I fear that describes it."

"For no cause?"

"Caprice. The same sort of caprice that made her——"

"I understand. She treated him shabbily then." Burr scanned the floor a moment, with something like a retrospective smile lighting the edges of his clean-cut lips. "I know that type of woman. . . I long ago marked the difference between Pamela and Charlotte. One is like a loose-clinging vine in a strong breeze; the other is like a tall, sturdy rose-tree, conscious of its strength, though careless of its beauty. . . Ah me! is there any type of woman, English, American, French, German, that I have *not* known and tested in my long, chequered life!"

He started out of his revery the next instant, and spoke once more to his companion with the electric vivacity and directness which he always gave to any theme that roused his sincere interest.

"As I said, Mark, these are my instructions. You depart to-morrow by the early-morning stagecoach. Meanwhile, your departure is to be kept wholly secret. There must be no farewells. You are simply forced to leave town. As you know, I am *ami de la maison* at the Verplanck home. I will drop in there after you have begun your journey." Here Burr rose, pushing back his chair. "Now," he finished, "is it a compact? I am forcing you into no groove of action; I am merely pointing to one which you can adopt or not, as you desire.

Yet if you ask me for farther details of my own intended course, I can only answer—'mystery'."

"But why 'mystery', colonel?" asked Mark, now rising also. "Since you have really convinced yourself that you have hit upon some happy exit from this distressing maze, why are you so determined to shroud in reticence the actual nature of your design?"

Burr pursed his lips inscrutably, and tapped Mark's breast with an outstretched forefinger.

"Because, my boy," he answered, with serious face though twinkling eyes, "I'm about to head a forlorn hope in your behalf. And I can't help preferring that you should poke fun at me after I have failed in it than disturb my old nerves by doubts and misgivings before I've set forth on my desperate attempt."

"In any case, dear colonel," answered Mark, with impulsive heartiness, "I should never dream of poking fun at a man whose abilities I so prize and admire!"

IX.

WHEN Pamela Verplanck received the letter that told her of Mark's departure for Boston, she gave a dismayed scream and looked on the verge of swooning.

"What is it?" cried Charlotte, terrified. And then, with amazement, she, too, read the truth.

"To go without bidding me a single good-by!" mourned Pamela. "And such a fearful distance off as Boston! Why, he will be two weeks getting there!"

"Horrible!" shuddered poor Charlotte; and in an uncontrollable paroxysm of suffering, she threw herself upon a lounge.

While she sobbed, Pamela

watched her with tearful eyes, through which sparks of suspicion began gradually to prick like needle-points.

"You're . . you're *very* over-come," she managed, with strangled voice.

"Oh, it's for your sake, Pamela," wildly fibbed poor Charlotte, drag-ging herself from the lounge. "I do so hope this news will not put you back. You were getting along so splendidly." Then she kissed Pamela's forehead, and smoothed her hair. "Let me give you your medicine, dear; it's . . it's time you took it."

"Oh, I've had medicine enough for one day!" And Pamela waved a limp hand toward the letter. "Your lips are cold, sister, and you're trembling. You feel this shock as much as I do."

"On your account, you know, dear."

"But he used to be so devoted to you."

"I've explained that. He—he felt the usual shyness and—and reluctance of lovers. . . Do you think you're less agitated, now? Take this."

Pamela took the medicine offered her. She lay back in her rocking-chair, and closed her eyes. She looked paler than for a good while previously, and in her face were reminders of former enfeeblement and prostration.

Charlotte, all this while, was struggling to be calmer. She succeeded, and chiefly for the reason that she felt certain Mark would soon send her some sort of explanation concerning his flight.

"It *is* a flight," she told her

father, when he returned from his office at dinner-time, one o'clock. "You remember what he said to us the night before last. And he never came at all yesterday. Oh, father, it's all very plain! He means to stay in Boston till Pamela is either out of danger or— dead."

Verplanck gave a great start. "But you say that she is now taking a quiet doze, and that you feel the shock will not be at all disastrous."

"I feel so—I hope so!" murmured Charlotte, as she helped her father to soup from the tureen of sprigged china looming before her.

"There's no doubt," said Verplanck, nervously crumbling his bread, "that this Boston invoice may cost the firm of Frankland,

Livingston & Vanderwater a good deal of trouble. They had had ominous advices regarding it some time ago, as commercial gossip informed me. Possibly Mark's vanishment may have been quite unavoidable, after all.''

'' I am nearly certain,'' said Charlotte,'' that he must have left some message for me.'' Her sweet eyes were full of mingled hope and doubt as she fixed them on her father's. ''And yet he may have feared that the fact of such a message would be discovered by Pamela.'' Here she trembled, drooping her gaze. ''Oh, perhaps I shall never hear directly from him through all the weeks of his absence! That will be torture!''

Verplanck sipped his soup as though it were nauseous. '' Charlotte,'' he at length sighed, '' I wish, now, that we had never persuaded him to attempt this deception!"

"Father! Was not our darling's life at stake?"

"It seemed so; . . and yet it may only have seemed: who knows? There is bitter injustice in forcing upon you, my child, so stern a trial."

"Never mind me," said Charlotte. "I shall try very hard to bear everything, for *her* sake. If she suffers no relapse I shall find my consolation there. In Mark's letter to Pamela he promises that he will soon write her again. Give the child three more weeks of increasing health, and she will have become her old self. Then we may break the whole truth to her, and though our tidings inflict great sorrow it will not be the sorrow that kills!"

"Ah," faltered Verplanck, in doleful undertone, "I shall hate that hour of revelation!"

"Not more than I shall hate it, father, heaven knows!"

Rather late that afternoon Dr. Wainwright called, and found his patient somewhat weaker, though not to any alarming extent. "I regret," he said to Charlotte, "that she should still rebuff the idea of going off into the country. Now is just the time when such a change would aid nature in working thorough restoration. I could but rarely visit her, of course, at Throgg's Neck, yet you could send me frequent bulletins of her advancement or retrogression."

"I will speak with her again on the subject," said Charlotte. "It is quite probable, doctor, that I may now induce her to go."

That evening, a little after supper, Aaron Burr dropped in. Pamela was upstairs, preparing for bed, since the doctor had still enjoined, above all things, a continuance of early hours. Verplanck received the guest, and for some time they spoke together. Then Charlotte came into the parlor, and there was more talk, intermingled, on the girl's part, with some very eager and almost breathless listening. And at last Charlotte said, with deep throbs in her voice,—

"Oh, Colonel Burr, so he has told you everything! And *you* are to receive the letters he sends me! It is all so strange! I did not dream he would rush away like this! But I see, now, that the strain was beyond his endurance. Father sees it, too—do you not, father? And will he write me often, Colonel

Burr? Did—did he leave me any parting message? If so, do you remember it? Could you repeat it *word for word?*"

"No need for that, my dear Miss Charlotte," said Burr, rising with his most graceful bow and handing her a paper.

Charlotte seized the paper with a stifled cry of joy, and hurried to one of the lighted candelabra. She read it through again and again (it was a passionate love-letter) with leaping pulses and glistening eyes.

"I greatly regret," Verplanck meanwhile said to Burr, "that Mark Frankland should have rushed off like this."

"Really, my friend," was Burr's reply, "every fresh day counted with him."

"Then you think it was entirely— business?"

"Oh, entirely."

"But he had time, colonel, to visit *you*."

"Ah, my dear Verplanck! surely you wouldn't compare a half-hour's chat with *me* to the wear and tear of interviews with *both* your daughters! And such differing interviews—each so trying in its special way!"

"I see. . . He has made you his confidant, has he not?"

"Yes; and a very safe one, as I hope you feel assured."

"Remember, colonel," said Verplanck, with the courtesy of the gentleman softly coloring his distressed mien, "that I have long been among your friendly supporters."

"Who than I should know it better?" broke from Burr, his voice charged with its own rich and peculiar vibrance. "You chose to join the small minority, and at a time when my foes and detractors were legion—as indeed they still remain! With all my poor wounded and battered heart, Verplanck, I thank you now, as I have more than once thanked you in the past.''

"Tell me," said Verplanck, returning the pressure of his guest's hand, "did not Mark Frankland show fear lest our beloved Pamela might be again imperilled by his sudden desertion?''

With the instantaneous alertness of the trained tactician, Burr made answer,—

"He had great trust in her coming recovery. He regarded her as now on the sure road to restored health.''

"Ah, how could he know?—how could he know?" Verplanck threw out, in dubious dolor.

"Nobody *can* know. But he surmised, he inferred." After a little pause, Burr quickly added, "The future, inexorably, is a blank; we can only paint there what gay or sad shapes we choose. Paint gay ones, my dear friend. It's always so much wiser. *I'm* painting them now."

"You, Burr?"

"Yes. I see the whole horrid complexity, but I feel certain there's a way out of it."

"What way?" sped the eager query.

"Bless me, man! As if I knew! As if I didn't merely hope!"

But Aaron Burr knew, all the while—or, with his characteristic sublime self-reliance, persuaded himself that he knew. Only, if Verplanck had offered to pay, there on the spot, every penny of his goading and omnivorous debts, very

probably he would not have disclosed (so strange was the wayward
and baffling nature of this unique
man) the why and wherefore of his
covert conviction.

X.

IN a few more days Pamela made no objection to leaving town. It was no longer a question of her going into the country for sanitary benefits, however. She could now not only take her walks abroad, but take them with her old springy step, and alone, had she so desired. One afternoon she did so desire, waving away Charlotte's offer to accompany her with quite a superb air.

"No, if you please. I want to write Mark to-morrow that I went out all by myself. How does my frock look behind? I don't wish it to be too long; it feels as if it almost touched the ground."

"Not at all, Pamela. And your bronze slippers show underneath it very prettily. But are you sure they're not too thin?"

"No; the weather's very dry. Now don't dream of following me, Charlotte."

"I promise you I will not."

But Charlotte watched her from one of the upper windows till she was hidden by the curving street. Pamela bore herself with secure serenity. She did not wish that any acquaintance whom she might meet should detect in her gait or demeanor the least sign of the invalid. It was a sluggish, gray afternoon, but she moved along with a positive buoyancy. Health was coming back to her, and in every fibre and vein she rejoiced at its gracious advent.

The hour was about five o'clock, and several people who had still remained in town, and who belonged to her small social world, came face to face with her. Three or four of these stopped her with ardent congratulations. One of them was an old lady with silky white hair, old enough to be her grandmother, and indeed a friend of that deceased ancestress on the paternal side.

"My dear child! I'm so glad to see you out," said the lady, kissing her.

"Thank you, Mrs. Van Rensselaer. It's very nice to *be* out, I can assure you."

"And all alone! *Isn't* it a little imprudent? My home is just here in Beaver Street. Won't you come in and let me give you a glass of blackberry wine? You look a .. a little tired."

But Pamela politely declined the blackberry wine, and sauntered onward. Her social world, as before has been said, was a small one. No marvel, then, that just as she came within sight of the big, breezeless trees of the Battery, Gerald Suydam should dawn upon her sight.

Pamela put out her hand in the prettiest way. She had once mercilessly snubbed Gerald, and knew that he had been in love with her to the verge of distraction when she did so. But now her humor was roseate and benign. Mark's departure had jarred on her most harshly, but it had not, after all, repressed the current of her reassertive health.

"I haven't seen you for a long time, Gerald," she said, amused by his evident confusion. "I hope you have been quite well?"

"Yes — yes — quite," floundered poor Gerald. "And I'm so glad *you're* well enough to go out alone like this."

"Thank you," she said, while his eyes devoured her face. A roguish impulse made her add, "I'm the least bit tired. Would you mind holding my parasol and strolling with me to a bench here in the Green? I think I should like to rest for about five minutes."

Would Gerald mind? He grabbed the parasol so tremulously that he almost dropped it. And literally he did not know what he was saying as he blurted forth,—

"It seemed to me that Mark Frankland's rushing off in such sudden style would make you worse again! I'm—I'm so glad, Pamela, that it hasn't."

In an instant the girl's eyes began to glitter strangely. But she kept her gaze away from Gerald as they walked on together. She knew very well that meeting her again in this abrupt style, and having her treat him so blandly, had gone to his head like some dizzying elixir.

"Has Mark Frankland told you, then?" she asked.

"Oh, yes! And I've suffered so on your account? But perhaps before he went he—he disclosed the whole secret. I think he *must* have done so. He wouldn't have dared leave on such a long journey as from here to Boston without letting you know how he'd been deceiving you."

By this time they were entering the little park. Pamela sank on one of the empty benches. As Gerald took his place at her side he gave a short, faint cry.

"You look paler. Are you feeling ill again?"

"No," replied Pamela, trying to smile. "What you said, however," she went on, measuring each word as though between lips that had somehow oddly stiffened—"what you said, a minute ago, Gerald, interested me. Please continue, will you not? I want to hear more."

"What I said?" fell feebly from Gerald.

He had, in reality, only the vaguest recollection of what words had just left him. He had been almost like a man talking in his sleep. He was not guilty of breaking his oath to Mark. The intensity of his agitation had betrayed him into breaking it—this, and this alone.

He stared helplessly at Pamela as she repeated, in quiet tones, every word of his recent pell-mell, automatic sentences.

Then, as she finished, his body

drooped weakly forward, and he began, in hurried fashion, to trace scrolls and flourishes with the tip of her parasol on the gravelled path at his feet.

"Give me that parasol," at length commanded Pamela, quite placidly, "and please at once explain to me what you have lately said."

XI.

AS he handed her the parasol, Gerald looked with despairing eyes into the face of the girl he worshipped.

"I—I've disgraced myself," he groaned. "I—I didn't know *what* I was saying! Pamela, you can't have forgotten how dearly I love you! And seeing you on a sudden, like this——"

"I understand," she put in, with icy repose. "You spoke of my being deceived by Mark Frankland. What did you mean by that?"

"Oh, you mustn't ask me! I—I don't even recollect that I said it."

"But you must tell me—you must tell me everything," insisted Pamela, grasping his arm.

And before they left the little park he had told her. He felt unspeakably guilty, and yet his sense of error was far less potent because of their after-talk than because of his first divulgence. As she rose and reapproached the gate, he said, following her,—

"Since I had begun, I was forced to finish. Mark Frankland will look on me as a perjurer, I suppose, and despise me as one. But the disclosure I made was involuntary."

"Yes, no doubt," Pamela said, vaguely.

"Ah," he brought out, with forlorn accents, "perhaps *you* despise me now!"

She shook her head in negation. "Not at all, Gerald. I should rather despise my own stupid credulity." She stopped, just outside the gate. "Thank you," she added, and gave him her hand for a moment.

"Are you going back home now?" he asked.

"Yes."

"May I not go with you?" he pleaded.

"You're very kind, but I . . well, I want to be alone for a little while."

"Can I come and see you?" he persisted. "Will you not let me come and see you some evening?"

"I—I retire quite early, Gerald. My doctor is still a good deal of a despot, you know."

"But in the afternoon, Pamela?"

"We are going into the country quite soon. . . We are going to Throgg's Neck."

"Dear old Throgg's Neck! What joyful times we used to have there! It was there, Pamela, that you first filled me with happy hope. And only such a short while ago! I can't tell you how often I've lived over in my dreams that one last delicious fortnight."

"Great changes come in short intervals, Gerald. Good-by." And Pamela, knowing that she was cruel, yet not wishing to be, struck northward at a quick pace. After she had gone a block or two, her progress slackened. She felt a little faint, and wondered if her old illness would now crushingly revisit her. "Why not?" she asked herself. "I have discovered that in their pity for me, in their wish to save me from death, they have made of me a most miserable dupe and fool!"

Walking slower, she soon caught sight of her own home. And then, with the passing of physical weakness, came upon her a shamed and haughty reluctance to let either Charlotte or her father learn of her disillusion. In reality, even the severe shock just dealt her had no power to throw her back upon a bed of sickness. She had been growing too steadily and radically better for any such result. This news might retard her full recovery, and plunge her into mental wretchedness, but fate had permanently snatched her from that dire collapse, and with revivified stamina she would go on living, despite the knowledge that she had been cozened and hoodwinked after this humiliating fashion.

These thoughts were flooding her mind as she now turned westward and entered Rector Street, moving parallel with the green lawns and gleaming grave-slabs that surrounded Trinity Church, then deemed a most grand structure since its re-erection in 1790 from the ashes to which it had been reduced in 1776.

It was pardonable in so young a creature as Pamela that she felt far more forcibly, just now, the sting of wounded pride than the heartache of bereavement. She was barely nineteen years old, and since childhood, as we know, had been the prey of many random and transitory whims. As the whole situation cleared to her she had not one residual qualm of resentment against either her father or sister. But indignation was sombrely gathering its energies, each fresh minute, with Mark Frankland for a cause. If they had wanted him to play the benignant hypocrite, that was no excuse for his having accepted such a rôle. She found herself tingling with shame and rage (both of which perhaps acted tonically rather than debilitatingly) as she slipped farther away from the broad brick front of her own dwelling.

"To think," were her passionate reflections, "that when father told him my secret he shouldn't have remembered he was born a gentleman, and at once have refused to deport himself otherwise! And then the gross falsehoods he uttered with such glibness! I might forgive him even those, but I *can't* forgive him the answers they drew from *me*. Those will go on mortifying me for the rest of my life—I'm sure they will!"

She stopped, now, in the bitterness of her bleeding girlish pride, and looked through the iron railings of Trinity churchyard at the placid graves of the dead. Perhaps the sensations that these awoke blent with memories of how near to death she had believed herself only a few weeks ago. Anyway, her savage arraignment of Mark became in a manner tranquillized, and she was just concluding that she felt calm enough to return and meet Charlotte, when a brisk voice sounded at her side:

"Miss Pamela! Can I believe it is really you? And quite unaccompanied?"

"Quite, colonel," she answered, shaking hands with Aaron Burr.

"All the more encouraging!" he exclaimed. "But I must not tell your people that I found you so dolefully employed." He pointed with a rebuking smile at the graveyard, but something in Pamela's look made the smile quickly fade.

She looked at him with a sudden

childlike wistfulness that soon changed to a more self-reliant gaze. As a little girl she had been taught to regard him leniently by the open leniency of her father. Then had come one of her causeless antipathies. And later, as we have seen, she had got to admire him altogether on her own account. She had fought battles for him with girl friends, had denied gloomy rumors concerning him, had praised his wit and grace and fine breeding. At the same time she knew he was a pariah, though she always had maintained that he was a social martyr as well. He had fascinated her as a personality, a presence, more than she knew. And now a strange yet natural impulse seized her—natural, at least, in a maid so volatile, alterant, and impetuous of temperament.

She would disclose to no one the tidings conveyed by Gerald! She would not breathe to any living soul a word of her new and mortifying discovery. She would pretend, when Mark Frankland returned from Boston, that she had not only outlived her ardent attachment, but had replaced it with another, more absorbing and intense. If her health did not break down again, if her vitality increased and throve, she would use every effort to dazzle and capture this elderly widower beau. He might respond merely in a self-flattered way; she already caught herself hoping that he would never dream of taking her blandishments too seriously. But she meant to exert them. It should be a vengeance of deceit for deceit. In his own coin she would pay Mark

back. She saw herself practising
before her mirror the glacial glance
that she would give him when they
next should meet. And if her pre-
tended heart-change did not plunge
a dagger of chagrin deep into his
masculine vanity, then she knew
of no weapon that could deal it
a more effective wound. All this
trend of resolve in her was hardly
measurable by time. "My good
Colonel Burr," she soon answered,
"is it queer that you find me staring into a graveyard when I was
expecting, only so short a while
since, to take up permanent lodgings there?"

"Don't speak like that, Miss Pamela! You pain me to the soul!"

"Ah," she said, very smoothly
and wooingly, "I should hate for a
moment to cloud your sunshine!"

"And why—pray, why?" asked

Burr, drawing nearer to her. Somehow, in a second, the girl perceived that he was handsomer than she had ever suspected. The afternoon was dim, but its light still stayed searching. She had always before seen him in rooms either where candles glimmered or curtains obstructed glare. Now it amazed her that maturity had left his tintings so fresh, and given not a single tired trace to the clear, white lids of his beautiful magnetic eyes.

"Why?" Pamela repeated. "Oh, because your cheerfulness has always affected me with such a holiday sort of feeling! I should hate to miss it when I met you." Here she smiled, and for an instant all hint of her convalescence fleeted; she had the air of a wilted plant that responds, leaf and stem, to some stimulant dewfall. "And I hope to meet it oftener in the near future. We are soon going to Throgg's Neck, and this summer you should not ignore the invitation father has often given you to come and make us a long visit."

Burr looked at her steadily for a moment. "My dear young lady," he said, "ever since I returned to my native land from those four years of exile, leisure has been for me a lost joy and struggle a continuous requisite. But now that you double the delights of your father's hospitality by promising me your own welcome as well, I am tempted to wish he would repeat his invitation, which I should surely accept in the teeth of every obstacle save illness or death."

He gave what to-day would indeed be called an old-fashioned

bow, bending low his body, lifting his hat with high-crooked elbow, and placing one hand just above his heart.

At the same time he was reflecting, "Bless us, could luck be more apposite? The first steps of my plan to pull poor Mark Frankland out of the mire have been smoothed for me as if by destiny itself!"

XII.

TOWARD the end of that same week the Verplancks left town for their country home. It was a great wooden house, that might have been far more angularly ugly while yet escaping such charge; for the lovely elms and chestnuts and oaks that shadowed its lawn, and the rocky shore, indented by coves of pearly sand, that you reached by only a short walk from its front verandah, were charms that made its architectural uncouthness an easy thing to forget.

Pamela had had a distinct relapse, after coming home from her walk that evening, and Charlotte kept accusing herself, in affectionate terror, of foolish indulgence. But the conviction of having been falsely alarmed soon cheered her.

"I fatigued myself a little; that was all," declared Pamela. "See if I don't bear our drive into the country as well as you do."

She bore it almost as well, if not quite. And when she got to Shady Shore (which was the name of their summer abode) she delighted her father by merrily informing him that he would soon be wishing Charlotte could only equal her plumpness and color.

"There's now not a grain of doubt," said Verplanck to Charlotte, "that she has taken a new lease of life."

"Yes, father," was the answer; "and yet her gayety has not always the right ring."

"How is that, my daughter?"

"I suspect that she is very angry at Mark, yet for some reason speaks of him as though she were not."

"H..m—yes," mused Verplanck. "Now that she is getting so well we must think about undeceiving her."

"Undeceiving her!" shuddered Charlotte. "Oh, father, I do so dread that! And yet it must come, must it not?"

"It certainly must, my child."

"Father!" Charlotte suddenly said, as though a fresh and pungent idea had occurred to her.

"Well, my dear?"

"Colonel Burr is coming, the day after to-morrow, to pay us a long visit. Why should we not induce *him* to break the news? Pamela is very fond of him, you know. We might ask him to use with her all

his wondrous diplomacy and adroit-
ness."

They did so, a short time after
Burr's arrival. But the colonel
managed to leave upon them no
more definite impression, in the
way of answer, than an inscrutably
amiable smile. He had his own
line of action to follow, not theirs.
A kind of social luminosity at once
diffused itself from him, in whose
rays his entertainers basked without
thinking how or why. This man,
who had survived the ruin of kingly
hopes, who had but lately been
pierced by the anguish of an adored
daughter's death and that of a treas-
ured grandson as well, who had
seen popularity and honor turn
avoidance and odium, could nevertheless deport himself with an
almost boyish blitheness, here in
the company of unprejudiced

friends. Even the servants of Verplanck, most of whom were blacks,
became his fervent admirers. He
was up earlier in the morning, by at
least two hours, than any of the
family, and took long rides on horseback, sometimes choosing an ani-
mal of doubtful temper, that his past
military experience and splendid
equestrian skill made him easily
subdue. In his radiant flow of
spirits there was no abatement, and
yet even the most frolicsome traits
of his humor and geniality were im-
bued with a dignity vague though
beyond dispute.

He told them (with inimitable
eloquence, pathos, and fun) of his
triumphs and failures, his successes
and defeats, during four years of
foreign life. It was not a common
thing to meet any one then who had
crossed the Atlantic, for our crawl-

ingly slow mail-packets had still left
us a nation of stay-at-homes. He
brimmed with amusing tales of privations and annoyances during that
thirty-five days' trip. He described,
with poignant satire and unfailing
mirth, the social London of 1808,
where he had met on terms of
intimacy the most important fre-
quenters of Holland House, where
he had hobnobbed with Lord
Bridgewater and Godwin and the
painter Fuseli and the young
Charles Lamb, and where he had
formed an undying friendship with
the wide-famed Jeremy Bentham.
"And all this while," he would
sometimes gaily add, "I was living on potatoes in lodgings whose
shabby locality I dared not name,
lest the Belgravian gentry who
heard of them might hold up horrified hands."

He recounted the most diverting tales of his struggles to escape from Paris, while a rigid surveillance guarded him there on every side, and the great, unapproachable Napoleon, now wedded to a Hapsburg princess and anxiously awaiting the birth of the King of Rome, refused him the audience he so eagerly craved. "Dukes and counts were, alas," he would say, "my constant enforced associates! They were forever measuring out yards and yards of red tape in which they both decorated and entangled me. I only wish some of it had been salable in those ticklish times; for there was an old woman, as I well remember, who kept a little stand in the Rue de Seine, and I had to make a *détour* in passing her for a whole week, because I owed the poor old soul two sous for a cigar."

Pamela's health was at length so reinvigorated that she insisted on accompanying Burr in an occasional horseback ride. "I'll promise to bring her home to you as fresh as when she started," he would say to either Charlotte or Verplanck. But by and by he would bring her home with a flush on her cheeks and a fire in her eyes that drew from her sister a faint though puzzled frown.

When Verplanck took a townward trip in the stagecoach, his guest did not always go with him. And when he did not, Charlotte found Shady Shore somewhat lonely, for the colonel and Pamela would spend longer and longer intervals in strolls and *tête-à-têtes*. Once Charlotte said, with a kind of chiding tone, to her sister,—

"Mark's letters from Boston

come frequently, I see. But you seem to dash off very brief answers, of late."

"Yes," replied Pamela, with chin at an airy angle and eyelids fluttering. "Life is so quiet here, you know, that I've scarcely anything to write him. Besides, he sends me so little news about his own doings. It seems very strange, certainly, that mere *business* should detain him east so long. There are quite as many pretty faces to be met on Boston Common, I'll venture, as on our own Battery."

"Oh, Pamela!" shot out Charlotte, unguardedly reproachful. "How *can* you believe him so——?" She stopped dead short, crimsoning to her temples. She had next her bosom, that very minute, an eloquent love-letter which Burr had yesterday received in his own mail from town, and had slipped into her hand when certain no prying glance was near.

The days went on, and Burr did not speak of departing. It was almost autumn, and some of the open fields were seas of fluctuant goldenrod, while sapphire knots of asters and thickets of glossy-beaded elders vied in color with the yellowing or reddening apples glimpsed amid rusted orchard leafage. A few neighboring Westchester residents, friends of the Verplancks, had interchanged visits with them since the coming of Aaron Burr. Others had expressed decided disapproval of his presence at Shady Shore, and refused to darken its doorways while he abode there.

Every summer three or four grand private balls would be given; and now, almost at the beginning of September, and still during the sojourn of Burr, it happened that the Van Wagenens, who owned a large and beautiful inland estate, five or six miles farther northward than that of the Verplancks, chose to entertain in their usual lavish way. Their ball was to be one of special note, and there was even a rumor that President Monroe might come on from the White Sulphur Springs to attend it. The Verplancks had received invitations, but none had been sent to Colonel Burr, notwithstanding his known presence at Shady Shore. There were imperative reasons why Varick Verplanck should, with at least one of his daughters, attend the ball. He had hoped that Burr would take final leave a week before the present date. But he had still stayed on, and had so often been seen in walks and drives and rides with Pamela that gossip had very palpably begun its condemning murmurs. Meanwhile the colonel had not attempted, as Pamela's father felt but too well assured, to enlighten his child regarding Mark Frankland's deceptive attitude.

"Pamela is an enigma," Charlotte had lately said to her father, feeding with fresh fuel the flame of his new disquiet. "I often think she has forgotten the very existence of Mark. There are times, father, when I fancy that Colonel Burr has deliberately tried to . . to turn her mind in another direction."

"Good heavens, Charlotte! 'you don't mean that he has dared, at his age, and with his shabby reputation (however undeserved it may be) to rouse any . . any *sentiment* in Pamela?"

But Charlotte swiftly denied the least security of conviction. All she stuck to was the undoubted fact that Pamela had now become deeply interested in Colonel Burr, and seemed ill at ease when an hour passed for her unshared by his company.

"If she were a boy," muttered Verplanck, half to himself, "I'd send her on a voyage round the world,—yes, as a sailor before the mast!"

"She isn't a boy, father," sighed Charlotte, "and she isn't any longer even a girl. She's become a woman, and a very complicated, mysterious, unmanageable one."

Two days before the Van Wagenen ball, Verplanck said at dinner,—

"You, Pamela, will probably care to go with me to Oakland on Wednesday evening. As your health, my dear, has now so splendidly reasserted itself, you should give some of your town friends the chance of congratulating you. Charlotte," he added, in a slightly chilled and strained voice, "will perhaps care to remain at home and have the colonel graciously let her beat him at backgammon."

" I'm sure," said Charlotte (thinking of her last letter from Mark, in which he announced his near return), "that I should greatly prefer such an arrangement."

"Father will have to go alone, then," affirmed Pamela, with her lips, now full and pink, a defiant pout. Then she turned to Burr, smiling saucily. "The colonel knows I would resent any such condescension at backgammon, but he may have the honor, that evening, of continuing with me his valuable lessons at whist."

"On Wednesday," said Burr, "I shall have returned to the city. Already," he went on, looking with directness at his host, " I have been tempted too long away from my dreary little office in Reade Street by the charming courtesies of this charming home."

Pamela's eyes fired, and her cheeks flushed. "No, no!" she exclaimed. "You are not going for a week yet! I made you promise so this very afternoon."

"You made me," corrected Burr, with a kind of smiling sadness, "feel very sorry that I could *not* so promise."

Pamela gave her head a mutinous toss. "There's no power that could force me to the Van Wagenens' ball," she said, looking straight at her father, "unless it were a question of putting me in a strait-jacket and carrying me there."

"Oh, Pamela!" reproved Charlotte.

"I mean every word of what I say! You and father can go, Charlotte, if you please. But while Colonel Burr was under our roof as our guest the Van Wagenens paid us a personal insult when they refrained from sending him an invitation. I, for one, shall pocket no such insult. Others of my family may do as they desire."

Burr sat perfectly still. His face, in the candle-light, which a soft breeze caused slightly to waver, could not have looked more motionless if it had been stone instead of flesh.

XIII.

AMID dead silence Pamela rose and left the table. It was not until she had disappeared that Burr said, addressing Verplanck,—

"You must know that I had neither expectation nor desire to receive a card for this ball. On Tuesday morning I had intended returning to New York. No one, as you must realize, can regret more than I do this unpleasant little development."

Verplanck bowed, though not cordially. He glanced, in a rather dazed way, at the table, as if to assure himself that the fruits served there betokened an end of the meal. Then he cast his eyes about the room, as if to make certain that the servants were gone. Soon he said, quite softly, to Charlotte,—

"My daughter, will you be good enough to leave Colonel Burr and myself together for a few minutes?"

Charlotte at once rose and glidingly disappeared.

Verplanck sat with bent head for several seconds. Then, meeting Burr's polite yet firm gaze, he began:

"Colonel, these later weeks have produced in Pamela, as you yourself have no doubt perceived, an immense change. If she were not my own child, and I were not overjoyed by her thorough recovery, I might call it a change almost ludicrous; and you know why. But for a still more powerful reason, as it pains me to tell you, I cannot call it that. The truth is, my friend, Pamela's

frequent appearances in your society—the spying and prying of
occasional visitors at Shady Shore
—possibly even the gossip of domes-
tics as well—have caused certain
unkind rumors. . . I trust you will
believe, Burr, that I speak with no
idle wish to wound you." And
here Verplanck rested his hand, for
a moment, on the other's arm.

"You could not wound me by
such a revelation," Burr serenely
answered. "I would not be the
hunted and maligned man I am if
calumnies and aspersions of all
sorts had not grown familiar to me
as the motions of hands and feet. . .
Well, now, since you have spoken
thus frankly, I will be equally frank
in return. But before uttering a
word of my intended confession, I
wish to make you another and much
briefer one."

"Confession?" murmured Verplanck. "I have never supposed
——"

"You have never supposed any but the most charitable things of me. You have painted me, as I am too guiltily aware, far less black than I deserve. But enough of that. The world, as you well know, imputes to Aaron Burr many atrocities of conduct." At this point, without the faintest theatric import, yet with much marked solemnity, he lifted his right hand. "But I swear to you that in spite of all slanderous contrary statements, I hold no crime more detestable than that of a woman's betrayal. I have never had but one child—my beloved and lost Theodosia! Yet if I had had a son, and he had brought dishonor upon a family by ruining a daughter of it, I would shoot him as I would shoot a dog !"*

Verplanck, paler than usual, slowly inclined his head. " Such avowal from you," he said, in smothered and uneasy voice, "was of course needless. Yet perhaps I may unwittingly have drawn it forth." His serious face now brightened inquiringly. " And the other 'confession' to which you referred ?"

Burr leaned backward in his chair. Deep thought seemed to absorb him for a short while; then, with an access of soft vivacity, he began to speak, straightening his posture, and at times waving slightly before him both delicate and shapely hands.

* See Parton's Life of Aaron Burr, vol. ii. page 308.

His first few sentences were graphic yet succinct. They told of Mark's visit, that morning, to his chambers, and of the young man's distressed entreaty for counsel in a frame of mind bordering almost upon frenzy.

"I then conceived a friendly idea of aiding him," Burr went on, "and that idea I have endeavored to carry out. It is difficult to speak of the idea: . . how shall I make it clear enough without having you think me a monster of vainglory? Yet that is something so different from what, in all justice, I want to have you think me! . . My dear Verplanck, I was the lover of my own sweet daughter. I never meet a young woman—seldom even a matured one—that I don't feel it in me to make her fond of me, to persuade her that I'm a vastly amusing and

engaging fellow. The odd part of
the matter is that this impulse
didn't die in me twenty years ago—
that it has not only survived in
me, but survived with unlessened
ardor and tenacity. They have told
shameful lies about me in my relations with women (notably in the
case of poor Margaret Moncrieffe),
but beneath all their lies a certain
stratum of truth has lain. I was
born with the power of making
women like me, just as some men
are born with the power of con-
trolling horses, others with that of
sailing ships. My power I might
have terribly abused, nor would I
for an instant claim that I have not
often used it with wayward folly.
But I have never, as my enemies
often state, steeped it in infamy. . .
And so, Verplanck, when Mark
Frankland bemoaned to me his

wretched situation, wrought by the recovery of a girl whose last hours he had been called upon to console with falsely amorous protestations—when he cried miserably to me, ' Colonel, here I am, the sworn and loyal sweetheart of one sister while bound by charitable falsehoods to another—another who will claim the fulfilment of every deceitful promise I have given her,' then did I, caring for the young man and pitying his unfortunate yet wholly blameless position, bethink me of a plan to save him."

" To save him, Burr ?"

" Oh, to pull him out of a hole, if you like blunter speech, my good man—to smooth and straighten the entire sad yet ridiculous turmoil. Do you guess, now, what this plan was ?"

"I think I do."

"*He* did not, nor would I tell him. I merely ordered him to prolong his stay in Boston." Here Burr lifted toward his lips the fragment of a cut peach that lay on his fruit-plate. Then he flung the morsel back again, rising.

"I don't think my plan has failed," he said, meeting Verplanck's look with his cool, blue, steady eye.

Verplanck rose also. "It may have gone too far."

Burr shrugged his shoulders. "At her age! The impression will doubtless fade in another month." His voice mellowed queerly, now, and a pensive gravity overspread his sensitive face. "Absence will do its sure work, just as it did in the case of Mark Frankland."

"There his absence, as you seem

to forget," said Verplanck, with gathering sternness, "was aided in its effect by your own presence."

"True. . . Well, I've done my duty as a friend in need."

"To Frankland—yes. But what about your neglect of it toward myself?"

The two men faced each other. Verplanck's eyes were very cold. From Burr's lips broke a glittering smile.

"How," he asked, "have I neglected it there? To disembarrass Mark was surely to disembarrass yourself—and your daughter, Charlotte, as well."

"You have been playing with edged tools, Burr," said Verplanck, haughtily and gruffly; "worse—you have been playing with fire."

"In desperate cases desperate remedies. I took them."

"And without my consent. Do you call that fair dealing?"

"As fair," sped the answer, "as for you to force a poor love-smitten lad like Frankland into acting the hypocrite."

Verplanck started. He caught from the table a crumpled napkin, held it an instant to his mouth, and then cast it down.

"I—I did that to save my child's life."

"And *I* acted as the friend and well-wisher of your other child's accepted husband."

"I deny your claim in so acting."

"Mark Frankland will justify it."

"How should that concern me?"

"In this way: you plunged Mark into an undeserved and cruel difficulty."

"From which you presumed to try and extricate him."

"At his request—yes. And you, by no means at his request, had presumed to place him there."

"These are your old lawyer's tricks," growled Verplanck, half turning away. "God knows I'm no match for you. Neither was the country, even though it tried you for treason—and a kind of treason no baser, after all, than this using of your wanton arts on my innocent girl!"

Burr folded his arms, with eyes blazing yet with composure immobile, and with manner melancholy though austere.

"You prove yourself a coward to reproach me with my past misfortunes," he said; and his voice, not seemingly raised, could have been heard farther than many a voice of more apparent volume. "But by insulting me while I am

your guest you strip yourself, besides, of all right to be called a
gentleman."

"Let me go, Charlotte!" came
a cry just beyond a half-closed
door.

"No, no, Pamela!"

"I will—I tell you I will!" And
Pamela, violently agitated, rushed
into the room. "Colonel Burr is
right!" she flung to her father.
"You have just insulted him—I
heard what you said. And often I
have heard you speak so differently!
'More sinned against than sinning'
—those were the words you often
used. And not seldom, too, have
you said of him that he was the
most slandered and unjustly per-
secuted of all the great—all the few
very great—statesmen our country
has thus far produced!"

"Pamela," stormily commanded

her father, "leave this room at once!"

"No; not till I've told you a few plain facts. I feel, though I'm not sure, that you have upbraided Colonel Burr for showing me kindness through these past weeks; I feel this because of certain hints you've dropped, father, full of bitter discontent. And now I'll inform you, fearlessly and openly, that Colonel Burr's presence in this house in no way concerned my change of feeling toward Mark Frankland — for on that change I'm sure you and Charlotte have passed comments together. . . Indeed, Charlotte admitted to me ——"

"Pamela!" her sister exclaimed.

"——admitted to me, only yesterday, that you had both wondered at my indifference, and the slight time

I gave to the answering of Mark's love-letters."

A burst of ironical laughter preceded Pamela's next words. "Love-letters, forsooth! All the time we have been at Shady Shore I knew the truth! I kept it hidden; in my frequent talks with Colonel Burr I was tempted to tell *him*, but I did not. Gerald Suydam, on the first day I went out alone after my illness, met me and made everything plain. Mark Frankland had confided to him your plot—yours and Charlotte's. It was a terrible deception—but I forgave you. I knew your love for me, your dread that I might die, had prompted it. And all this time you have thought that Colonel Burr's goodness in deigning to treat me civilly and cordially was my reason for caring less and less about Mark. No—disgust and con-

tempt were my reason! I may
be wrong, and I may judge him
with partiality and prejudice, but it
seems to me that he should have
told both you and Charlotte it were
better to lose a daughter and a sister
than to take so hypocritic a means
of saving her life! And his falsehoods, as I now firmly believe, *never*
saved my life. Nothing saved it but
the will of nature, the turn for the
better in my malady, whatever that
really was. And so you wrong
Colonel Burr most cruelly, father,
when you even suspect that he has
had the least share in my disregard
of Mark. Scarcely ever, in our talks,
have we even mentioned his name.
Oh, I did not hear much that you
said, but I heard enough to sicken
me with horror and shame. *You* to
sneer at his 'lawyer's tricks,' when
I have heard you, again and again,

praise his legal abilities as glorious!
You to accuse him of using wanton
arts on an innocent girl, when every
new moment of his companionship
has taught me more and more to
respect while I admired him!..Oh,
colonel," she continued, still keep-
ing her eyes on her father's face,
now ashen and deeply perturbed,
"I am certain that father will make
you amends for the dreadful insult
he has just paid you! I am certain
that his sense of honor——"

And there Pamela paused. In
the spot where Burr had stood was
vacancy. He had quietly vanished.

XIV.

AT once, after leaving the dining-room, Burr went to his own apartment upstairs and gathered together all his possessions—all very simple and easy of redisposition within his trunk—employing that speed and dexterity which were half due to his early military life and half to the years of hardship which had succeeded it. Then he pulled the bell-rope, and held a little consultation with the black servant who soon appeared. In that crisp, concise form of speech which he knew so well how to adopt, Burr made it clear that he wanted a conveyance as soon as possible, and one that should bear himself and his lug-

gage to a certain small hotel about
a mile distant, where he meant to
pass the night. When the man
departed he plainly understood and
had promised carefully to obey.
Every servant at Shady Shore was
now Burr's sworn friend; his power
of attracting inferiors by an occasional kind word or smile was a
minor feature of his almost historic
personal charm.

When sure that his order would
be carried out to the letter, and that
within a half-hour his trunk would
be waiting for him in a vehicle near
one of the smaller lawn gates, Burr
went downstairs and stood for a
moment in the dimmish hall. He
had meant to leave the house forth-
with by its rear door, but seeing that
the front door at the end of the wide
hall was open, and feeling the cool,
salty breeze that pulsed below its

lintel, he remembered that he would have ample leisure to steal out by this mode of egress and get a farewell glimpse of the wooded shoreland which recent associations had taught him to treasure.

All prepared for final departure, he moved past two or three lamp-lit rooms, looking neither to right nor left. Then came the gloom of the high-columned portico; then the descent of its steps, and then the waterward slope of the lawns. Off beyond the Sound a full moon had lately risen, but at first he had only a sense of its elfin glamours up between the interspaces of the many dark and stately trees. Presently he came to the water's edge, where a full tide lapped the rocks and a splendid pathway of rippled silver broadened from the shadowy Long Island shore. Between two great tree-trunks there was a rustic seat which he well knew. He sank into it, and watched the magnificent lunar glow and listened to the drowsy, voluminous cadences of the soft wind among the bowering trees. It was a perfect night—one of those few exquisite ones which our rather churlishly hot American summers are apt to spare us. Burr, who loved nature with the soul of a poet, cherished all its grandeur and sweetness at their full, rich worth.

"Well," he thought, "I have striven to do a friend service, and have received scorn for my wage. Has it often been otherwise with me, through all my curious, twisted, calamitous life? No doubt the things I have done that men call evil things have mostly, if not all of them, sprung from just this sense of disesteemed effort, underprized purpose, misvalued energy. . . Let that dear, wilful girl say what she chooses—I *did* snatch her from the woful results of her own unfortunate sentiment. It has not been Gerald Suydam's disclosure; it has been my own steadily worked-out method of consolement, distraction, mentally and emotionally alike.''

''Colonel Burr.''

He rose quickly as his own name mingled itself with the rustlings of the trees. Then he saw Pamela standing near him.

''You—you are going away,'' she said, her glance having gathered in this fact by a swift measuring survey of his altered dress. ''I saw you from my window upstairs. You came here—I know why—to bid our pleasant haunts a silent farewell.'' Her eyes were shining wildly in the sylvan dusk of the place. She was bareheaded, and clad in a light simple frock whose high-waisted fashion of the period became her frail yet rounded shape, and blew backward in the marine night-breeze with a fairy effect of gossamer pliancy.

"Father was very wrong—infamously wrong—to speak as he did, and you are right to go. Yet I feel you cannot be angry—you have long borne too much unmerited insult for that; you are only grieved to the depths of your soul—your noble and patient soul! But still, father will make you amends—I am certain of it. Unless ——" And here Pamela suddenly paused.

"Unless . . ?" Burr questioned, with an involuntary repetition of the girl's own word.

"Unless you are willing that I

should share with you your future.
I know this is madly bold of me—
I know that you may despise me
for it. But to-morrow I could meet
you—if you are really going to-
night, as I know you are—and then,
provided . . . ''

''My dear Pamela,'' said Burr,
drawing nearer to her, as she again
paused, ''what are you saying?
Share my future, child? How
could you possibly share it but in
one way?''

''That is the way I mean,'' she
gasped. Her bosom rose and fell in
quick pulsations below her delicate
bodice. She looked like a young,
sweet, fiery angel, with her scintillant eyes, and her parted lips, and
her wind-waved floss of hair, and
her fluttering draperies.

''That is the way I mean,'' she
again said, each word in a sort of

sobbed staccato. "The one way—
the honorable way! I—I pity you
so deeply! You have told me much
of your past life, and you have
always spoken of its weakness, its
failure, its wrongdoing. But I have
seen more than you chose to show
me, and I have fancied that you
might care to let me stand between
you and your vilifiers—not making
the least sacrifice—far from that—
but helping where I could, and
healing where I could, and always
giving you the devotion and as-
suagement and comfort of which
you have unconsciously taught me
to believe you so worthy!"

Burr stood quite still as her plead-
ing impetuosity became silence.
He saw that she had stretched both
hands half-way, as if to meet the
response of his own. But for a
while he did not take them. It

was only a brief while, and yet its interval was packed for him with a mighty temptation.

His advanced years had brought with them none of the feebleness they bring to many another man. This was more than proved by his marriage, fourteen years later, to Madame Jumel, a woman whom he did not love, and in wedding whom, at Fort Washington, just fifty years from the time that he had wedded the mother of his adored Theodosia,* he committed what was almost the crowning folly of his strange career.

And now, before one of his susceptible nature and splendid physical hardihood, there rose this temp-

---

* The same clergyman, a Dr. Bogert, who had performed that earlier ceremony, united him, fifty years later, to Madame Jumel.

tation of immense potency. To
humor Pamela's wish he had only
to make an acquiescent sign. To-
morrow she might become his wife
—she, the daughter of Varick Verplanck, a man widely honored, a
merchant of conspicuous wealth
and influence, the friend of Clay
and Adams and Randolph, one who
had but to lift his hand in order to
find himself mayor of the city or
governor of the State. Here would
be rehabilitation, past dispute. The
returned exile, the despised outcast,
the erstwhile fugitive, would have
achieved incalculable social gain.
Many might still refuse to countenance him, but many more would
regard him on totally altered terms.
The chance, the opportunity, was
priceless. And was he not capable
of bestowing on this enthusiastic
and impassioned girl a fondness and

fidelity which would shield her against disappointment, repentance, ennui? Might she not become an old man's darling in every sweetest, most reverent, most enviable sense?

But the picture had its reverse side. Such a match, on her part, must prove, after all, a fatal mistake. And, besides, she was too young to be trusted with the arbitration of its wisdom or unwisdom, its policy or impolicy, its prudence or rashness. No; he might indeed have "gone too far," as Verplanck had lately said; but he would go not a step farther. He had alienated her from Mark, and had taken that course solely through an impulse of friendly aid. Here his task should end. A few recent weeks of this girl's existence he had made his own. Her future was like some frangible crystalline thing which honor and conscience forbade him to handle, forbade him even to touch. "Honor and conscience in an Aaron Burr!" so many would cry scorningly, if they knew. But they should not know. They had enough of his alleged criminalities to wreak expression upon. Let them glut their spleen with those.

"Pamela," he soon said, very gently, taking both her hands, "I promise you always to guard with my life, as a sacred confidence, your tender and lovely disclosure. But for your own sake, dear child, I answer that the granting of your wish would be on my part a disloyalty, a treachery, even a cowardice as well. I say this boldly, though hating to wound. And what hurt I inflict will, believe me, cease more speedily than you dream. Your days are bright with promise and hope—mine are darkened with the shadows of approaching old age, apart from those of bereavement, poverty, and ruthless popular dislike. With all my soul I thank you—I dare not trust myself to say more. . . . I shall never forget you—shall watch your joys with a great gladness hereafter, and grieve deeply for your sorrows—which may a merciful God lighten, if He does not wholly avert!"

For a moment Burr's lips drew nearer to hers. Then, as with stout effort, he receded a little, still clasping her hands. On each of these he pressed two or three quick kisses, and where the kisses fell, big heavy tears fell, too.

Then he dashed the tears away with either freed hand, for they blinded him in the dimness. And without another look at Pamela, who stood pale and tremulous, he hurried off among the enshrouding trees. . .

Later, he found that the vehicle, with his trunk inside it, waited in the precise spot where he had desired it to meet him. Entering, he was borne to the inn at which he had purposed passing the night, spent there many sleepless hours, and finally, early on the following morning, was driven by stagecoach to New York.

*   *   *   *   *   *

Two days afterward he sat in his office. The time was a half-hour or so before noon. On his desk lay a letter, which he had repeatedly read. It was from Varick Verplanck, and it teemed with contrition and apology.

" Kind old friend !" Burr at length murmured, aloud, while he slowly refolded the letter. "As if it needed so much fine rhetoric to make me forgive you! And as if I didn't realize, five minutes afterward, that you never meant a word of your insult!" He gave a long, slow sigh.

"Ah, Varick Verplanck, if all the stabs I've got from my fellow-men had only drawn as little blood as yours did, how much happier and braver and thankfuller a man the present moment would find me!"

His low words had hardly died away when Mark Frankland, with tumultuous lack of ceremony, burst into his office. "My dear colonel! Give me *both* your hands to shake! I'm so glad to see you again—and thank you!"

"You arrived home to-day, Mark?"

"No—last night at about nine, miserably tired with that endless jolting journey, as you may well believe. Now that we can sail by steam, why can't we ride by it?"

"We shall, in a short time. Note my words—before five years have passed, that brilliant Englishman, George Stephenson, will have perfected his engine, and blessed the century with a priceless boon. . . You received my letter when you reached home?"

"Yes. Ah, colonel! And *that* was your 'plan'! Oh, you sly wizard!" Mark broke into a roar of the blithest laughter. Then, seeing the sadness on Burr's face, he swiftly added,—

"But I do trust there's been no —no disastrous complication?"

"No . . none."

"And Pamela does not guess the truth?"

"She does not guess that *I*—well,

you understand. Regarding the
other part of it, Gerald Suydam, as
I wrote you yesterday, broke faith
with you and told her of your merciful duplicity."

"Gerald Suydam—yes!" cried
Mark, his face clouding. "Whom
should I run against this very morning, before I had gone half-way to
father's office, but that same tanta-
lizing young person! One minute
he implored my pardon for letting
the cat out of the bag to Pamela,
and the next he spoke with jealous
wrath and scorn of you."

"He had heard certain rumors,
then, from Shady Shore? Well, he
may set his excited mind at rest.
Some day, if he prove himself a
wise and patient wooer, he may
win Pamela for his wife, after all.
It's by no means certain, however.
His way to matrimony will be a

rough one, I promise him. It is not paved with ease and peace, like yours and Charlotte's."

Mark's face brightened again. "Ah, colonel!" he exclaimed, leaping up from the chair into which he had thrown himself, "if Charlotte and I marry and have children, I should like to fling defiance at all your foes by calling our first boy Aaron Burr Frankland!"

"I'm sure you would not be capable of doing anything so unfatherly," said Burr, shaking his head, with a grim smile. Then, after a moment, the smile grew limpid, genial, characteristic. "Call him by another name, my boy. Call him after the woman whose life brought me more happiness than all my successes, and whose death has dealt me more pain than all my other sorrows combined."

"You mean . . Theodosia?" said Mark Frankland, softly.

"Yes! Call your first boy, if God gives you one—Theodore!"

THE END.

ELECTROTYPED AND PRINTED BY J. B. LIPPINCOTT COMPANY,
PHILADELPHIA, U. S. A.

www.ingramcontent.com/pod-product-compliance
Lightning Source LLC
Chambersburg PA
CBHW030831270326
41928CB00007B/992